TROPICAL AFRICA

Political Map

Names of cities over 1,000,000 are capitalized

National capitals — Leopoldville
Other capitals — Zanzibar
Political Boundaries
Railroads

0 50 100   200   300   400   500 Miles
0   100   200   400   600   800 Kilometers

LIFE WORLD LIBRARY

TROPICAL AFRICA

OTHER BOOKS BY THE EDITORS OF LIFE:

LIFE WORLD LIBRARY

TROPICAL AFRICA

by Robert Coughlan

and The Editors of LIFE

A STONEHENGE BOOK

TIME INCORPORATED   NEW YORK

COVER: Mounted guards
carrying swords and flagstaffs
parade during ceremonies
marking the independence of the
Federation of Nigeria in October 1960.

ABOUT THE WRITER

Robert Coughlan, who wrote the interpretive text for this volume of the LIFE World Library, has been a reporter and editor for Time Inc. for more than 25 years. Since 1949, he has served as a wide-ranging LIFE writer. He is the author of biographies of William Faulkner and Maurice Utrillo, and has won numerous citations for excellence in reporting both domestic and foreign affairs. In 1960 he received the Distinguished Service Award of Sigma Delta Chi, the national journalism society, for "Black Africa Surges to Independence," a LIFE article in two parts which was produced after a 15,000-mile journey through Tropical Africa which took him to 19 countries. In 1961 he traveled to most of these countries and a number of others as well to gather additional material for this book.

Contents

TIME INC. BOOK DIVISION

Editor
NORMAN P. ROSS

Copy Director   *Art Director*
WILLIAM JAY GOLD   EDWARD A. HAMILTON

Chief of Research
BEATRICE T. DOBIE

Editorial staff for "Tropical Africa"

Editor, LIFE World Library	OLIVER E. ALLEN
Assistant to the Editor	WILLIAM K. GOOLRICK
Designer	BEN SCHULTZ
Chief Researcher	GRACE BRYNOLSON
Researchers	RUTH GALAID, PAULA VON HAIMBERGER ARNO, REBECCA CHAITIN, MARY ELIZABETH DAVIDSON IRENE ERTUGRUL, NANCY JONES, RENÉE PICKÈL. NAN ROTHSCHILD, LOUISE SAMUELS, HELEN R. TURVEY, LINDA WOLFE
Picture Researchers	MARGARET K. GOLDSMITH, JOAN T. LYNCH
Art Associate	ROBERT L. YOUNG
Art Assistant	JAMES D. SMITH
Copy Staff	MARIAN GORDON GOLDMAN, CAROL HENDERSON, DOLORES A. LITTLES

•

Publisher	JEROME S. HARDY
General Manager	JOHN A. WATTERS

•

LIFE MAGAZINE

Editor   *Managing Editor*   *Publisher*
EDWARD K. THOMPSON   GEORGE P. HUNT   C. D. JACKSON

•

The text for the chapters of this volume was written by Robert Coughlan and for the picture essays by Walter Karp. The following members of the LIFE Magazine staff helped in producing the book: Eliot Elisofon, Alfred Eisenstaedt, Carl Mydans, Larry Burrows and James Burke, staff photographers, and Doris O'Neil, Chief of the LIFE Picture Library. Valuable assistance was also provided the staff by Lee Griggs and Philip Payne of the TIME-LIFE News Service and by Content Peckham, Chief of the Time Inc. Bureau of Editorial Reference.

Introduction

No one who has watched the events of the past few years in Africa could fail to be excited and concerned. The coming of age of the new African nations, which was given impetus in 1957 with Ghana's independence and reached a climax in 1960 when no less than 17 new African states emerged, is one of history's great political developments.

As I said in 1960 in a speech before the United Nations General Assembly, the achievement of independence by these nations constitutes a dramatic expansion of freedom. It strikes a responsive note in the hearts of the American people, for we achieved our own independence less than 200 years ago. Freedom, as we have learned, imposes a heavy responsibility: a responsibility to individual citizens at home and to the community of nations abroad.

The people of the United States have a special bond with Africa, not only because we too have trod the path to freedom, but because many of our citizens are of African origin. Americans through the years have shown their interest and their concern for Africa and its peoples by their participation in the establishment of the independent Liberian Republic, by the founding of missions and schools over much of the African continent and by generous contributions of their economic resources and technical skills to Africa's development.

In recent years Africa has become a critical quarter of the globe, an area where political developments from one week to the next have threatened to plunge the world into war. As we have followed the amazing sweep of African events—the violent upheaval in the Congo and the growing pains of the emergent nations—our hope as Americans has been that the people of Africa could work out their own destiny in their own way without sacrificing their freedom.

In preparing this volume Mr. Coughlan and the Editors of LIFE have performed a service that is unique. They have, through the medium of vivid words and superb pictures, cast a new light on an area that must be illuminated if we are to keep pace with the great rush of human events in this vital area.

CHRISTIAN A. HERTER
former U.S. Secretary of State

At a U.N. General Assembly session in New York, the Nigerian delegation closely follows the proceedings. Today 24 nations from

Tropical Africa are seated at the U.N. In 1955 there were two.

1

Panorama of an Emerging Land

THERE was a time not so very long ago when Tropical Africa evoked thoughts only of the exotic and adventurous: of lions and savages, of great, green, greasy rivers and perhaps even of Tarzan swinging on a jungle vine from tree to tree. Then suddenly the tom-toms stopped, and all that one heard was a cacophony of political slogans (Free*dom!* . . . One Man, One Vote! . . . Indepen*dence!*) and the names of parties and candidates, punctuated by intermittent gunfire and an occasional scream. When finally the jungle parted, it was to reveal a line of black men no longer in loincloths but in business suits, and no longer carrying bundles on their heads but with attaché cases in their hands, filing into the delegates' lounge of the United Nations to have brandy and cigars and devise the next strategic move of the newly-emerged African bloc of nations in the affairs of the world.

This is all too fast for the mind to follow. How can the two images even be related, let alone be superimposed to make something coherently whole?

Of course, both images are distorted to start with. Sadly, there never really was any Tarzan. Quite as sadly, a good many of the new nations, for all their official paraphernalia of legislatures, armies, airlines, cargo fleets, postage stamps, currencies and diplomatic receptions, are almost as illusory as Tarzan, and some of them are unlikely to last as long as his legend. And yet both also are to a considerable extent real. Tropical Africa has indeed been primitive—one of the most backward large areas in the world—and, except as a cockpit for competing colonialisms, it was until recently a political void as far as the outer world was concerned. Today, although still largely primitive, it is bubbling with progress and ambitious hopes, and its leaders are listened to attentively in the world. The casual newspaper reader in the U.S. is likely to feel that there is a new African nation almost every month; indeed, the onrush of independence throughout Tropical Africa has in recent years been overwhelming. In 1960 and 1961 alone, 19 new nations came into being. All this has come about in an incredibly short time. Where time had meant nothing, it now is almost visibly the fourth dimension.

If the sheer breakneck pace of these events is enough to leave the observer (and numbers of Africans) disoriented and rather dizzy, its effects are compounded by nature. In his *Travels in the Congo*, André Gide wrote, "In this immeasurable land, there is no center, the lines go in all directions, everything is without limit," and complained of "its enormity, its shapelessness, its lack of decision, lack of conformity." That was 30-odd years ago, but the modern traveler often feels the same peculiar sense that he has lost track of time, place and identity. We are dealing with something vast, amorphous, disjunctive and infinitely complex.

Hence it is necessary to put up some boundary markers, guideposts and warning notices.

Africa's dramatic transformation in recent years is revealed below, the second map showing the continent as of December 31, 1961.

1950

"Tropical Africa" is a term of convenience rather than of precise geographical measurement. To be sure, the area under discussion here is unquestionably "tropical," since nearly all of it is between the Tropic of Cancer and the Tropic of Capricorn—that is, between lat. 23.5° N. and the same latitude south of the equator. The general location is important because of its effect on the climate, which affects so much else. But the two lines have no particular meaning in themselves, whereas in either direction there is something else that does. In the north there is the Sahara, an immense natural obstacle that has tended to keep North Africa more or less separate from the rest of the continent. In the south there is the man-made barrier of *apartheid,* which recently has made the Republic of South Africa and its administrative fief, South-West Africa, even more separate from the mainstream of African life and affairs. The area under inquiry—Africa south of the Sahara and north of the Republic—includes Madagascar, now called the Malagasy Republic, which lies 250 miles off to the southeast. The whole of Africa covers about 11.6 million square miles and the area we have chosen about 8.5 million square miles. The continental U.S. without Alaska would fit into Tropical Africa nearly three times.

There are arguments about whether Madagascar ought to be thought of as part of Africa: it is so big—1,000 miles long and up to 360 miles wide—that it comes close to qualifying as a subcontinent. Then there are arguments about where the Sahara ends and hence whether the phrase "south of the Sahara" has any meaning. And there are other arguments: indeed, Africa has emerged so recently that almost everything about it is still being defined.

This being so, the interpretations and judgments here are a synthesis of many sources. Almost any statement about Africa is subject to qualification. Only those that seem particularly important will be noted as we go along. The reader should therefore equip himself with a set

United Nations Trust Territories are labeled U.N.T.T. Dependent nations are listed in italics, independent ones in capital letters.

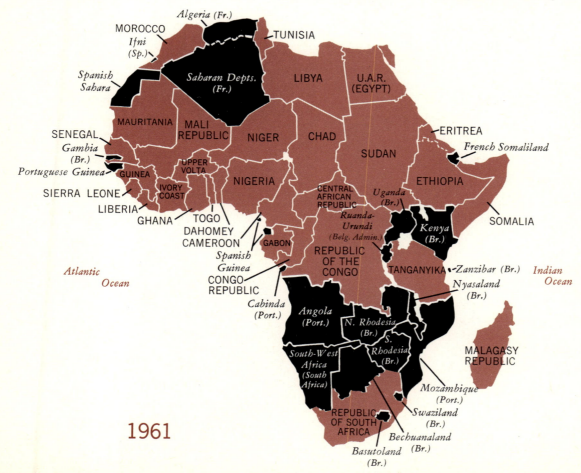

1961

of qualifiers—"probably," "perhaps," "more or less"—and mentally splice them into anything that sounds like a generalization.

Not all aspects of Africa will be taken up here. The purpose of this book is to take what is most representative and meaningful and use it to create a comprehensible general picture rather than to give a full and exhaustive analysis. To avoid repetition, we shall be referring to Tropical Africa most of the time simply as Africa. Where the whole continent is meant, it will be clear from the context.

The best way to see Africa—in fact the only way to see it in a single lifetime—is to travel a great deal by air. This enables one to take in the countryside in all its variety; whereupon, having spotted something that looks particularly interesting, one can descend for a closer view or come down at the nearest airport or landing strip (of which there are hundreds) and spend whatever time is needed to satisfy one's curiosity.

FOR the rest of this chapter—and from time to time thereafter—the reader should imagine himself air-borne. The aircraft may as well be an advanced model that can fly very high and very fast but also can hover in mid-air and land and can take off vertically. It contains, along with the usual survival kit, a compact reference library so efficiently cross-indexed that pertinent facts and figures will pop out at a moment's notice. Thus equipped, the reader can address himself to the question "What is it really like in Africa?"

"Geologically," wrote George Peter Murdock of Yale University in what may well be the most concise sentence ever written about the African continent, "Africa consists largely of a single rigid block of rock of marine origin laid down perhaps 200 million years ago and later uplifted." This uplifted rock now consists of a single enormous plateau surrounded by a strip of beach and coastal plain which varies in character all the way from utter desert to oozy swamp. Often, especially along the west coast, it is bordered by lagoons, which look nothing at all like the flowery blue-water lagoons of

storybooks and travel posters but instead are wide, dark and immensely long. When surrounded by heavy forest growth, as along the Ivory Coast and parts of what used to be the Gold Coast, they are quite forbidding to behold. Flying along these shores for mile after countless mile, occasionally glimpsing a human in a dugout canoe or a partially cleared patch with a few grass huts, but otherwise seeing only the water and the vast, sullen, black-green forests, one can imagine what a psychological barrier a coastline like this must have presented to the early Europeans who sailed this way.

WHERE there are no sand bars or lagoons, the surf crashes against the shore in heavy, white-crested swells. For vast stretches, there are no good natural harbors. Sometimes one will find a pretty cove, or a stretch of beach safe behind a sheltering reef with sand so fine and light that it looks like lemon cake-mix. Sometimes also there is a cliff or a hill, and at one point on the west coast rises the improbable bulk of Cameroon Mountain, 13,300 feet high. Otherwise the west African coast is mostly featureless. But it is not neutral. There is a sort of lethargic, low-key foreboding about it, a feeling one gets of resentment against intrusion. It is disturbing; it prickles the nerves with atavistic fears. The east coast has a somewhat more hospitable look. There are coral reefs and sandy beaches with no mountains or forests; the air seems clearer and the water bluer.

In the days when the world was mostly unexplored, the normal method of finding out about the interior of a place was to go along until one came to a river of some size and sail up it. The bigger the river, the bigger the watershed and the more one could learn: Hernando De Soto, when he found the Mississippi, had much of the present-day United States within his reach. The African coastline contains the mouths of a multitude of rivers, but there are two difficulties about them. Most of the larger rivers here egress through deltas in labyrinthine ways, with sand bars and shifting mudbanks which are likely to bewilder and endanger the traveler. Moreover, although many are navigable for great distances along their middle courses, few of them are of much help in getting from the coast into the interior, for if they are big and long enough to be potentially useful they usually are blocked by rapids or waterfalls. The falls and rapids on the Nile, the Congo and the Zambezi are among the greatest natural sights of the world.

Victoria Falls on the Zambezi is wider than Niagara Falls and more than twice the height. Its spume rises far into the sky like a cloud of smoke from a forest fire, and then it descends to the earth as mist, keeping the vegetation at the top of the chasm dripping wet. When the sun shines there are rainbows, multiple and immense and so brilliant that they seem palpable. They move with the light, fading and emerging and forming again at different angles and in different sizes, so that sometimes one can actually see where they begin and end.

The plateau gives Africa more than a third of the potential hydroelectric power of the world: about 259 million horsepower, more than that of North and South America, Europe and Australia combined, and this is a fact of the greatest economic importance, for although the area has great mineral resources, most of it is poor in the ordinary energy sources—coal, oil, natural gas —that have enabled other places to develop industrial wealth. Only a tiny fraction of this water power has been developed so far, but it offers the prospect that Africa could become one of the world's greatest industrial regions.

THERE is something else about the plateau that should be noted: it is tilted. It rises in the east to a mean altitude of about 8,000 feet in Ethiopia, the highest country, and it reaches high average levels—anywhere from 3,000 to 6,000 feet—in a broad belt that arches south and west from Kenya through the Rhodesias and Angola. In most of western Africa, on the other hand, the elevation is less than 1,500 feet and in many places falls away to mere hundreds of feet. These are facts of great political importance, because one of the main determinants of

temperature in the tropics—and thus of human comfort, and thus, in turn, of where European settlement has occurred—is altitude. A convincing demonstration is to fly from the sultry coast of Kenya, where few Europeans have settled, up to the capital city, Nairobi, which lies a few hundred miles inland and more than 5,000 feet higher, and which at the turn of the century became a notable English outpost. The weather in Nairobi during most of the year is like a Maine summer—pleasantly warm during the day but downright chilly at night, so that a light sweater is welcome. Taking the whole area, the eastern highlands average between 15 and 20 degrees cooler than the coastal strip.

THE highlands of eastern Africa have another advantage: they contain some of the world's loveliest, most peculiar and most spectacular scenery. There are great mountains here: Kilimanjaro, Meru, Kenya, Elgon, and the Ruwenzori and Virunga ranges. The Virunga range contains active volcanoes; what is more remarkable, since these are the tropics, some of the other mountains have permanent glaciers. Kilimanjaro, the highest (19,340 feet) peak in Africa and taller than any in Europe, has one and Mount Kenya (17,040 feet) has several, although it straddles the equator, a fact which offers the interesting possibility that one might stand on the equator and get frostbite, or for that matter freeze to death.

Here also are the Rift valleys. There are two of these huge, troughlike depressions. The Eastern, or Great, Rift is about 4,000 miles long. Actually it begins far north of the African continent in southern Turkey, runs south through Syria, forms the water-filled declivities known as the Sea of Galilee and the Dead Sea, and enters the African continent at the southern end of the Red Sea. From there it turns southward and extends all the way to Mozambique, where it enters the Indian Ocean south of the Zambezi River. The other, the Western Rift, lies several hundred miles away and runs roughly parallel for most of its 1,250-mile length before veering eastward to join the

Great Rift in northern Nyasaland. Both vary from 30 to 50 miles across and are hundreds to thousands of feet deep.

The depths of these rifts form catch basins for water from the surrounding highlands and mountains, and the result is a double chain of long narrow lakes. Lake Tanganyika, the largest of them, is 400 miles long (about one half the length of California); its surface lies at 2,500 feet above sea level and its bottom lies at 2,200 *below* sea level. Together with Lake Victoria, which occupies a shallow basin between the rifts and is, after Lake Superior, the largest body of fresh water in the world (about the size of Ireland), these comprise the great lakes of Africa. Besides being marvelous to look at and decidedly important in the lives of the millions of Africans who live near them, they rank among the natural wonders of the world, although comparatively few people outside Africa even know their names: Rudolf, Albert, Edward, Kivu, Tanganyika and Nyasa.

Another discovery the traveler makes as he moves about is that Africa, far from being all jungle and forest, has every gradation of landscape from stinking swamp to bone-dry empty desert. The legendary jungle of Tarzan exists all right, and it can be as rampantly fructuous and quite as menacing as the legend has always had it. Winston Churchill, in *My African Journey,* summed up marvelously well the feeling one gets being inside such a growth.

ONE becomes, not without a secret sense of aversion, the spectator of an intense convulsion of life and death," Churchill says. "Reproduction and decay are locked in infinite embraces. In this glittering equatorial slum huge trees jostle one another . . . slender growths stretch upwards—as it seems in agony—towards sunlight and life. . . . Every victor, trampling on the rotting mould of exterminated antagonists, soars aloft only to encounter another host of aerial rivals, to be burdened with masses of parasitic foliage, smothered in the glorious blossoms of creepers, laced and bound and interwoven with interminable tangles of vines and trailers. Birds are as bright as butterflies; butterflies are as big as birds. . . ."

There is an estimated third of a billion acres of jungle and rain forest in Africa—but it is relatively a small portion of the land, only 6 per cent or so, mostly along the west coast and in the Congo basin. From this fulsome extreme the forest thins out until it turns into the most characteristic of African landscapes, the savanna—undulating grasslands dotted with individual trees and occasional groves, often quite tranquil in appearance, like a great open park. But this in turn shades off into sparser country, with scrubby trees and bushes and mottled patches of bare earth, and then into desert lands speckled only with thorn bushes and other tough growths and scarred by gullies and dry sand rivers; and at the final extreme, rocky, sandy, barren desert. This "true desert" is found in only a few places and accounts for only about 2.5 per cent of the area. But desert and semidesert, land that is agriculturally worthless except for light grazing, account for about a quarter of all Tropical Africa.

THE transition from forest to desert has little to do with the quality of the soil. Most African soils are poor, some being merely poorer and some better than the rest, with only an occasional area of rich fertility. The forest is largely in the lower reaches, and the savanna and the scrub and thorny stuff—all the undependable interwoven growths that are known colloquially as "bush"—ordinarily come at higher levels and roughly in the order mentioned. But what really determines the density of vegetation is not the altitude; it is the rainfall. Until the traveler has seen it for himself—until he knows the smell and feel of it, the way it can crumble a modern apartment building into moldy decrepitude in a few years, or the way the lack of it can make the air so parched that it seems almost brittle, causing laundry to dry stiff as a board in 10 minutes—it is difficult to understand what rain means to Africa. This is one place where "D'you think it'll rain today?" can be a brilliant conversational gambit, a question fraught with complicated nuances and fascinating possibilities.

There are three main rules of thumb to keep in mind about African rain. One is that it is seasonal. Being tropical, the area has no real summers or winters (at the outer limits there is an annual temperature range that seldom exceeds 10°) but instead has rainy and dry seasons. Near the equator there usually are two of each, with the rainy seasons arriving near the two equinoxes (late March and late September), whereas toward the Tropic lines they merge into a single rainy season and a single dry one. Vegetation and life in general tend to keep time, waxing in the wet and waning in the dry.

THE second rule is that the amount of rain varies inversely with the distance from the equator: the closer the wetter, and the farther the dryer. At the Tropic boundaries the single rainy season lasts only about four months, and when it does rain, the fall is moderate.

The third rule is not to put much faith in the other two. They are riddled with so many exceptions, due to the inter-reactions of ocean currents, terrain, winds and assorted perversities of nature, that the only safe generalization is, "It all depends." The city of Conakry, the capital of the Republic of Guinea on the western "Hump" of Africa, gets about 12 feet of rain a year. To be out in a really first-class rainstorm here is rather like walking around at the bottom of a lake: visibility is only a few feet, and it seems as if anyone who carelessly took a deep breath probably would drown. Yet at the same latitude on the other side of the continent in Somalia, on the eastern "Horn" of Africa, the precipitation at certain points is only a few inches a year, entirely in the form of dew. The wettest spot in Africa is a place called Debundja, on the slope of Cameroon Mountain: more than 33 feet of rain falls on it every year.

Similarly, and for no predictable reason, a semidesert area such as that around Lake Rudolf (the northernmost of the Great Rift's major lakes), which ordinarily gets about 10 inches of rain a year, may get that much in a fortnight. A rainy season may come weeks early, weeks late, or perhaps not at all. The latter occurred in Kenya in 1961: the "long rains" of March to June failed to arrive, with disastrous results for the wild animals; grazing areas and water holes dried up and thousands of them died. The "short rains" of October to December thereupon arrived in such insane force and abundance that many animals that had not died of thirst died of drowning. Bridges and roads were washed away, dams burst and power stations were wrecked. The disaster spread through much of East Africa, until an estimated million people were in danger of starvation. They had to be saved by air-drops of food and an international relief program.

Which is why, in Africa, it is so boring not to talk about the weather.

It is these eccentricities of weather as much as the "average conditions" of a place that determine what sort of vegetable, animal and human life it will support. Obviously, if there were many such drought-flood cycles as that of 1961, there would be nobody left to enjoy the benefits of Kenya's generally attractive climate. At least in a broad way, however, it should be possible to draw a coherent botanical, zoological and even population map of Africa in terms of mean annual rainfall. The African rain forest of lore and legend and the kinds of life it supports need about 80 inches of water a year, which is a lot of water. And so it goes through the gradations of "dry forests" and savannas, with about 20 inches being necessary for land cultivation if one wants to get a reasonably good yield of even a rather hardy grain.

TAKING it all together—the sultry swamps and backwaters and quagmires of the rainy parts, the cruelly unrewarding lands of permanent drought, along with the gullies and rocky protrusions and the leached-out, burnt-out, worn-out soils—probably a third or more of Tropical Africa has offered its inhabitants little more than a marginal existence. And this is something that the traveler soon feels, whether he looks down at Africa from the air or travels on the ground: so much of it is empty and lonely that he can easily sink into melancholy as he contemplates all this vast hopelessness.

As a matter of fact, there is an odd sense of near-vacancy about a good deal of the rest of it. There are splotches of intensive cultivation —places like Iboland and Yorubaland in Nigeria or, in east central Africa, the magical former kingdom of Ruanda, with its hillsides all neatly terraced and its luscious pastures looking in the rainy season as if they had been freshly upholstered in bright green plush. But elsewhere evidences of human life sometimes are hard to find: a hut here and there, an occasional village. There is a feeling, traveling in such countryside, rather like the desolation one feels on entering an unexpectedly empty meeting hall. One gets an uneasy urge to follow anything that looks like a path, and to poke around and call out, "Where *is* everybody?"

IT is all the more startling, therefore, to encounter Africa's cities. They rise from the jungle and bush like volcanic mountains sticking up from the sea. And they are real cities in the modern western sense, with some populations in the hundreds of thousands and broad avenues and office towers that glisten in the sun. Dakar, Lagos, Leopoldville, Luanda, Salisbury, Lourenço Marques and Nairobi have business and residential sections that would do credit to almost any moderate-sized city in the U.S. or Europe.

They testify to Africa's potential wealth. They were built because somebody knew a way or felt sure there would be a way to make a profit big enough to compensate for all the hazards of climate and terrain: in big-scale agricultural enterprises involving export produce such as palm oil, peanuts, coconuts, coffee, cocoa, rubber or sisal; or in mining operations involving gold, diamonds, copper, iron, uranium, bauxite, zinc, mica, tungsten, manganese, tin, columbite, tantalite or other strategic minerals. They have acted like magnets, drawing hordes of Africans from the countryside—the fortunate few to settle in well-planned developments,

but the majority to live in ever-swelling slums. The cities, with their air-conditioned baby skyscrapers and festering social problems, symbolize a great deal about Africa's probable future.

But present-day Africa, for all of its being so unmistakably an area in transition, is better symbolized not by the city but by the village, not by the tower suite but by the one-room hut made of mud and thatch. Of the estimated 175 million people in Tropical Africa, fewer than 10 per cent live in communities with as many as 5,000 people.

IF it is true that urbanization is growing, that town ways are spreading into the countryside, that few Africans have remained wholly unaffected by western civilization's products— in a range extending from the fly-specked colored advertisement torn from a magazine and tacked to the wall of a mud hut, to the medical diploma hung on the wall of a doctor's office— it is equally true and more pertinent that the vast bulk of Africa's people live where their fathers and forefathers lived and do mostly the same things in much the same ways. There is a tiny educated elite, a larger but still very thin layer of skilled workers; increasingly there are traders, handicraftsmen or practitioners of other specialties; the rest get their sustenance directly from the earth as tillers or pastoralists, fishermen or hunters. Most of them—on the order of 85 per cent—are still illiterate. Their political horizons are generally bounded by the village or tribe: the idea of nationhood, or that they themselves are part of a nation, remains largely an abstraction. If they have heard of the United Nations, it is ordinarily a mystery to them and less interesting by far than the vagaries of wind and weather.

In short, the great majority of Africans not only live close to nature—they are themselves, in most essentials, still a part of that whole landscape of lion and baobab tree, ant hill and anteater, orchid, snake, smoke rising, water falling, sunlight and moonlight, in which everything is somehow involved with and conditioned by everything else.

In central Africa, the bodyguards of the King of Katoa stare balefully out of bloodshot eyes. Their scars are ritual marks of manhood.

Variety Wrung from a Faceless Terrain

Variety in Africa is largely man-made. On a landscape that is vast, monotonous and vaguely repellent, the most striking features are the works and ways of men. Mud metropolises sit defiantly on wastelands. The splendors of the Orient are duplicated incongruously on sun-seared plains. Festooned with villages and kingdoms, and with a bewildering array of customs, Africa offers many surprises—and perhaps the greatest is that men have thrived here at all.

PLUNGING CANYONS cut into a fertile plateau in the highlands of Ethiopia. Dotted with mean huts and criss-crossed by mule paths, the table-top land stands 8,000 feet above sea level. Here a monarchical civilization has been in existence for 2,000 years, cut off from the rest of Africa by sheer mountains and waterless deserts.

POISED GOATHERD, adorned with ostrich feathers, cloaks himself in the studied elegance characteristic of his people, the fiercely independent Masai of East Africa.

STRAINING BOATMEN of the Wagenia tribe heave their paddles furiously against the rapids of the lower Congo in a tremendous dugout canoe manned by 80 crewmen.

ROYAL AIDE of a Nigerian emir is swathed in robes and turban, a costume introduced by Moslems and now widespread in West Africa.

MOUNTED TRAIN of chiefs and court dignitaries passes in review (*right*) at Kaduna, capital of Nigeria's predominantly Moslem north.

PARAMOUNT RULER of a Ghanaian tribe (*below*) is borne on a litter by his pages. The drums behind him are symbols of his authority.

DANCING MAIDENS of the Miango district in Central Nigeria shuffle and chant in unison to celebrate a marriage in their village. Their only adornments are bright ker- chiefs, leafy boughs and girdles of cord meticulously wrapped about their waists. Such meagerness of dress is reserved solely for unmarried girls; Miango women now

wear western clothing after they are married. The marital tie itself is a complicated one among the tribes of the region. A woman can "divorce" her husband simply by eloping with a man from another village. Should she return to her first husband's village, however, she is accepted back as one of his wives without further ado.

ROBED RETINUE of Sudanese Moslems is assembled
outside a private palace in Khartoum, which is decorated
with neon lights in honor of the Moslem New Year.

WALLED CITY of Kano in Nigeria has been a Moslem
metropolis for some 500 years. Its 130,000 inhabitants
still profit from trade with trans-Saharan camel caravans.

TRADING CROSSROADS, the streets of Zanzibar Town
house merchants from every continent. The town is the
capital of Zanzibar island, domain of an Arab sultan.

2

A Slowly Yielding Society

THE common synonym for Tropical Africa is "Black Africa"—*Afrique Noire*. It is a term that has in a sense been legitimized by us-age, just as "the white man" and "European" are usable terms for people whose skins range through all sorts of hues and relative degrees of lightness. *"Nous sommes les noirs*—We are the blacks," Africans say proudly, and they too en-compass a broad variety of hues. Some of them are almost blue-black; their skin has a rather opalescent gleam, and when they wear white or a combination of bright clear colors the effect is dazzling. From this extreme, skin tones range through black-browns, browns, grays and tans all the way to some as light as those seen in parts of southern Europe and the Middle East.

And as one soon discovers, complexion is only one of the ways in which the peoples of this Black Africa differ in appearance. They vary in height, in the proportions of their bodies and in their facial features—as much as the Eu-ropean peoples differ. As James Cameron has said in *The African Revolution:* " . . . the dis-tinction between an Ashanti from Ghana and a Xhosa from the Cape is at least as obvious as that between a Sicilian and a Finn."

The common denominator is that nearly all of them are Negroid—that is, they contain, in varying degrees, the physical characteristics associated with the Negroid racial stock. Some anthropologists would go no further: for since all "races" are composites and there is no such thing as a "pure race," they feel that any attempt to classify people in racial terms is automatically doomed to inconsistency. Moreover, not only is anthropology an inexact science, but there are great gaps in anthropologists' knowledge of Africa.

NEVERTHELESS, faced with the fact that people do differ in appearance and that different types tend to cluster and form recognizable groups, scientists have used the concept of race as a working tool. In the definition approved by a UNESCO committee of anthropologists and geneticists, race is "a classificatory device providing a zoological frame within which the various groups of mankind may be arranged and by means of which studies of evolutionary processes can be facilitated." Efforts are being made to classify Africa's peoples by physical characteristics, but detailed and precise information is lacking. Africans have been classified linguistically, but there is, of course, no correlation between language and physical appearance. A Hopi Indian in Arizona, for example, and a highlander from Scotland both speak English, but they are strikingly different physical types. Similarly there are African peoples who differ widely in cultural and physical attributes but speak the same language. In the present exceedingly dim state of knowledge, therefore, any groupings that can be made are necessarily only rough approximations. With this proviso in mind, we can proceed to describe some of the more commonly recognized categories of Africans. All figures and terms apply to "typical" adult males.

The members of one distinctive group, the Pygmies, average about four feet six inches in height and 88 pounds in weight. Their skin is not black but yellowish-brown and often is covered with downy body hair. They are forest dwellers, and in earlier times they probably roamed the whole forest belt that extends across the middle of the continent, an area that is almost as large as the continental U.S. west of the Mississippi without Alaska. Small scattered groups of them are still there, leading their traditional lives as hunters and foragers, traveling about in bands of three to 30 families. Intermingling with other peoples has created "pygmoid" groups here and there, and these folk—taller in stature and variously changed, but with the pygmy strain still recognizably present—may number about 100,000 to 150,000. Of the "typical" Pygmies, there now are only about 35,000 to 40,000.

The Bushmen are somewhat taller, averaging close to five feet, and are distinguished by their extraordinarily wrinkled skin and slitlike eyes. Once they occupied immense sections of eastern and southern Africa, but they now can be found only in a few southern areas, particularly the Kalahari Desert. Estimates of "typical" Bushmen surviving today vary from 10,000 to 50,000. These two groups, the Pygmies and the Bushmen, are relatively distinct; some authorities would even call them races or subraces.

CAUCASOID racial elements have come into Tropical Africa from two major sources. One was the Hamite (or Hamitic-speaking) peoples who, from very ancient times, inhabited the northern and eastern parts of the continent. The Berbers of the Mediterranean coast (the Barbary Coast), the early Egyptians and the early occupants of the Ethiopian plateau were Hamites, and from these areas migrations took place with important consequences that will be discussed in the following chapter. The other source was the Caucasoid peoples from the Arabian peninsula known as Semites. But since that term has confusing connotations, they will be referred to here as Arabians or simply as Arabs.

Negroes, who comprise the major physical type in Tropical Africa, most commonly have been divided into the following categories:

The West African Negroes (sometimes called Guinea Coast or "true" Negroes) are generally about five feet eight inches tall, with skin that ranges from dark brown to blue-black. They have very little body hair, and their head hair is dark and kinky. Their noses are broad and are more or less flattened; their lips are thick and tend to turn outward. They inhabit the larger parts of the independent countries of Senegal, Mali, Upper Volta, Niger, Guinea, Liberia, Sierra Leone, Ivory Coast, Ghana, Togo, Dahomey, Nigeria and Cameroon, and the still-colonial territories of Gambia and Portuguese Guinea.

THE Bantu peoples, another Negro category, tend to be lighter than the West African Negroes and also shorter and less flat-nosed and thick-lipped. They vary considerably among themselves, some groups being lighter, some darker, and so on; in fact the only consistent factor that distinguishes them from other Negroes is that the languages they speak have characteristics that are common to them and to no others. According to C. G. Seligman, the University of London's pioneer in African ethnology, "Even more simply the Bantu might be defined as all those 'blacks' who use some form of the root *ntu* for human being; with the plural prefix this becomes *bantu* (Bantu), i.e., the men . . . whence the term under which the whole great group has passed into anthropological literature." The Bantu occupy most of the lower half of the African continent.

The Nilotes (pronounced "nye-lotts") live in east Africa—particularly the great lakes region of Ruanda-Urundi, Uganda—and the upper valley of the Nile. Compared with the two foregoing groups, they tend to have thin lips and narrow, high-bridged noses. Moreover, everything about them seems to have been elongated—they are tall, slender and long-headed, and it is common to see men of six feet or more. Some experts feel that there are traces of a Caucasoid strain in the Nilotes, probably a North African influence, but the available evidence suggests that they are merely a localized variant of the Negro. Southern Nilotes include the well-known Watutsi (or Tutsi) from Ruanda-Urundi, whose male dancers—seven

feet tall many of them, with spears and lavish feathered headdresses—have appeared in movies such as *King Solomon's Mines*. They include also the Masai (who are sometimes called Nilo-Hamites) of Kenya and Tanganyika, the proud and intractably independent nomads who paint themselves from top to toe with red ochre that is mixed with grease, and drink the blood and milk of their cattle.

The Malgache, as the five million inhabitants of Madagascar are called, are an ethnic mixture. They are predominantly Negroid, with Arabian, Melanesian and Asiatic overtones.

In the course of migrations, wars, border raids, slaveholding, concubinage and peaceful neighborly intermingling there has been a tremendous amount of fusion, resulting in all sorts of mixtures and surprising genetic outcroppings. As Laurens van der Post tells in his account of the Bushman, "Though gone from the land, he still stalked life in the mixed blood of the coloured peoples as subtly as he ever stalked the multitudinous game of Africa. He was present in the eyes of one of the first women to nurse me, her shining gaze drawn from the first light of some unbelievably antique African day. Here a strain of Bushman blood would give an otherwise good Bantu face an odd Mongolian slant, there turn a good central African black into an apricot yellow. . . ."

AGAIN, in the easterly and northerly regions of Africa great numbers of people regard themselves as being of Arabian descent, although to the dispassionate eye it may be hard to tell them from the surrounding populations. On the island of Zanzibar, for instance, which for centuries has been ruled by Arab sultans but lies near the African coast, it is rather startling to meet so many Arabs who look like Negroes and to find them committed in politics to the "Arab" cause versus the "African."

All this overlapping should not be taken to mean that African ethnic groups have lacked a sense of their own unique identity or have lacked pride in it. As William O. Brown, Professor of Sociology at Boston University, and

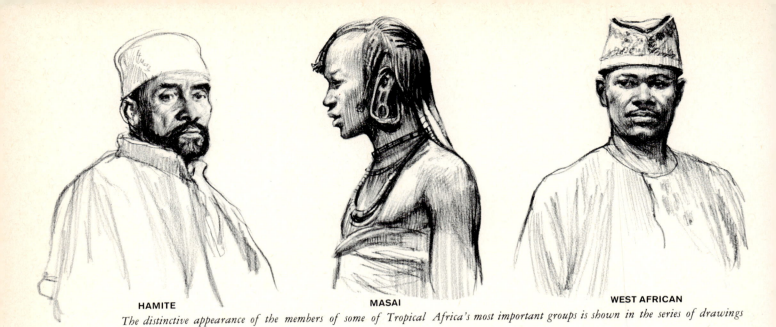

HAMITE   MASAI   WEST AFRICAN

The distinctive appearance of the members of some of Tropical Africa's most important groups is shown in the series of drawings

social researcher Hylan Lewis point out, "This is not to say that the indigenous inhabitants show no consciousness of race differences, or that race never reinforces social distinctions." The Africans are relatively free of color consciousness, but they are human, and racial problems have occurred in Africa as in other parts of the world.

EVIDENCE that racial tension may have existed a long time ago in the Nile valley, for instance, is suggested by a boundary marker which the reigning Pharaoh of Egypt caused to be erected at Semna, near the second cataract of the Nile, in 1879 B.C. (economic and political factors undoubtedly also played a part in the situation):

"Southern boundary, made in the year 8, under the majesty of the King of Upper and Lower Egypt, Khekure (Sesostris III) who is given life for ever and ever, in order to prevent that any Negro should cross it, by water or by land, with a ship (or) any herds of the Negroes; except a Negro who shall come to do trading in Iken or with a commission. Every good thing shall be done with them, but without allowing a ship of the Negroes to pass by Heh, going downstream forever."

But while "race" cannot be dismissed as an aspect of African life, it seldom has been a primary factor. Again quoting Brown and Lewis:

"Though race is not generally the basis for group prejudice and solidarity, or a source of tension and conflict among Africans, inter-group hostilities are prevalent. In Africa, as in other parts of the world, the sentiments associated with *we* and *they* are powerful . . . sharp distinctions are made between those who belong and those who do not."

The prime determinant of *"we* and *they,"* and in most other ways the thing that has mattered most to the African in his ordinary day-to-day life, has traditionally been his tribe. Today, although the scene is changing and allegiances to political parties, trade unions, religious sects and other modern groupings have grown, this is still largely the case. The politics of the new countries are still bound up intimately with tribal allegiances. And African politics very often makes no sense at all unless one knows the tribal factors that are involved.

The most important thing to know about tribalism is simply that there is so much of it—so much that the number of tribes is difficult to estimate. A tribe has been defined as a group of people who have cultural and political unity, similar customs and usages and who are descended from a common ancestor; according to this definition, there are at least 700 tribes. However, if one allows for all the variations that divide members of a general group into more or less autonomous subgroups,

PYGMY BANTU BUSHMAN

above. It should be noted, however, that tribal intermixing and other factors have reduced the proportion of "pure" physical types.

then the number would be in the thousands.

Language is the most obvious variant. In Nigeria alone, there are some 250 more or less distinct "languages"—hence there probably are at least as many tribes. Tribal domains are so intermixed that sometimes villagers living only a few hundred yards apart speak languages that are mutually incomprehensible, and have to communicate with each other through bilingual members. On the other hand, more than half of Nigeria's 40 million population is accounted for by only four tribal groups, each of which has a language that is understood by all within the group: the Yoruba, the Ibo, the Hausa and the Fulani.

THE same situation exists in a general way throughout Africa, with some tribes the size of nations and others the size of villages. Perhaps the smallest of all tribes is the El Molo of northern Kenya, a wistful little band who live on the barren black volcanic desert shore of Lake Rudolf. They subsist almost entirely on fish and hence are dying off from deficiency diseases, but they refuse to move to better land. When last counted they were down to only 97.

The El Molo refuse to move because they like where they live and because they are attached to the customs that their peculiar existence has evolved. This, really, is the essence of tribalism. A tribe lives by its traditions. No matter how the traditions may have originated, or whether in the view of outsiders they are sensible or insane, admirable or deplorable, they are good in themselves because they are what the tribe does—what the tribe *is*. They comprise a discipline which the African absorbs from earliest infancy and to which he tends to conform without question. If for some reason he should lapse it is not merely the apparatus of tribal government that chastises him—it is the even weightier force of unanimous public opinion. By imposing its own particular set of customs and standards of behavior on its members—and no nonsense about it—the tribe is thus the main instrumentality for law, order and respectability (according to its own criteria) in Africa.

Some of the tribal customs are so important that they define a whole mode of existence. The El Molo cannot imagine *not* being a fisherman. The neighboring Karamojong is a herdsman and cannot imagine being anything else—certainly not a fisherman, for to him fish are an unclean, tabooed food. Both the El Molo and the Karamojong would find the behavior of the Suk in the hill country of northwest Kenya peculiar; they do no fishing or cattle herding but are simply sedentary farmers, staying in one place and growing crops. Other customs are as minute as the Nandi rule that when meat has been eaten, milk may not be drunk for 12 hours, and then only after salt and water have been taken. Few customs are entirely unique. Like one of the most visible outward symbols of tribalism, the "tribal mark"—formed by cutting the face in a pattern and allowing the cuts to scar over—they are, for the most part, variations on some fairly common theme. (In urban Africa "marks" are going out of style now, but many of today's African leaders have had them from childhood.)

Whatever its customs may be, the tribe will have ideas about what is right and proper and will cherish them as its own. These cover all important aspects of life from birth, nursing and weaning through adolescence, marriage, parenthood, old age and death, including the disposal of the body and the attentions that are to be paid to the departed spirit. In novel or ambiguous situations where no ready answer exists, one is provided by the tribal leaders, who in turn are guided by the spirits of the ancestors and by the tribal gods.

THUS, so long as a man remains within the matrix of tribal organization, he has a clear idea of what he is supposed to do and when and how to do it, and what he can expect his fellows to do. If he leaves the tribal area and goes to live elsewhere—in one of the new towns, say—the corollary is that, being used to living by this close-knit code, he is likely to be uneasy without it. Almost instinctively he looks for a group to join: a political party, a church, a trade union, a tribal association of earlier émigrés—something that will restore his sense of belonging to a group and sharing a common purpose.

This urge to combine with others, to accept and take comfort in group standards, is characteristic of all levels of traditional African society, from that of the tribe all the way down to that of the family. Indeed it begins with the family; the tribe is in many ways an extension of African family "togetherness." To understand how the structure fits together, therefore, it will be useful to follow an African through some of the major landmarks of his life.

From the moment of his birth he is involved in a vast web of relationships, their degree of complexity depending in part on his father's economic status. If this is reasonably good, his mother is likely to be only one among several wives and, accordingly, he probably will have a number of full and half-brothers and sisters. Polygamy is permitted or outrightly favored by most tribes, for reasons that have been well summarized by anthropologist G. P. Murdock:

"Africans have discovered means of making the institution work to the satisfaction of both sexes. No woman lacks a male provider. No . . . wife has trouble finding a helper or baby sitter in time of need. Since the first wife normally enjoys for her lifetime a position of superior authority and prestige, every woman knows in advance of her marriage what her future status will be and has no fear of being superseded. Since men almost universally establish each of their wives in a separate dwelling and endow them individually with land and livestock, sources of friction are reduced to a minimum. Custom normally requires the husband to treat each wife with equal consideration, to eat and sleep with each in regular rotation, so that no married woman suffers public humiliation through any overt manifestation of favoritism. In consequence of these cultural adjustments, missionaries seeking to institute monogamy in African societies frequently encounter their strongest opposition from the women."

THE position of the male parent at the center of things does not necessarily mean, however, that he always has the decisive voice in all family affairs, or indeed that the children even bear his name. In some tribes it is the mother's family that counts in calculating family ties and descent. In such "matrilineal" societies it is the mother's brother who has final authority over her children. There are many variations of relationship and residence, but in all cases the family is a group enterprise. Characteristically it consists of the husband and his one or more wives, his unmarried children, and his married sons with their wives and children —a group that might number in the dozens and would live in a cluster of huts in a compound. In turn, these individuals would have crisscrossing family ties with similar groups in neighboring compounds, so that often villages or even whole sections of the countryside are, to all intents and purposes, one big family.

The family, whatever its size, is part of a clan —a sort of superfamily whose members claim a common ancestor and who (in some parts of Africa) also believe that they have a special relationship to some creature or object in nature. This is their "totem," and they venerate it and use it as the name and symbol of their clan, becoming known as the Lion Clan, the Crocodile Clan and so forth. Clan membership runs into the tens of thousands in the larger tribes; yet the sense of family relationship is so strong that marriages between men and women of the same clan are banned as incestuous.

THE second great landmark for the African, next in importance only to birth, comes during adolescence when he undergoes formal initiation into adulthood and into the mysteries of the tribe. Not all tribes have these "rites of passage," and of course the rites themselves vary enormously. Most characteristically, however, youths who have reached puberty since the previous ceremony are taken as a group. Afterward there is a close fraternal bond among them. They comprise an "age set" and pass through all the stages of tribal life together, being graduated at the same time from the status (among the Masai, for instance) of junior warrior and arriving together, many years later, at the status of governing elder.

In most tribes the initiation into adulthood is celebrated with elaborate ceremonies. Circumcision often takes place as a part of the initiation, and in some tribes the ceremonies for girls include clitoridectomy. Instead of performing genital operations, some tribes knock out or pull out one or more teeth; still others do both.

Again, at marriage, which is the next major event in the African's life, individual wishes tend to be subordinated to the interest of the group. Among most tribes young people may choose their marriage partners, but tradition requires that the match be approved by the families of the man and woman involved, by the village elders and chief, and the groom still must pay the "bride price"—money, goods or services to the family of the bride. This does not mean that he actually buys her—she does not belong to him in the sense of being a chattel, and she can leave him if he abuses her— but is a recognition of the fact that her services are valuable, and that the loss of these services to her own family requires compensation.

Bride prices have been going up for many years all over Africa, and this is one reason why so many young, single men leave their villages to work a few years in the mining settlements and the new towns. Money is also needed for schooling, for taxes, for European goods such as bicycles—the changing times have created many newly felt needs—but perhaps none is felt more keenly than is the necessity of saving enough money to get a wife. The sojourning African adds his bit to the social problems of town life while he is there, and then contributes to the weakening of tribal values when he comes home again with his town sophistication.

MUCH more could be said about these values. But the general pattern of African society can be seen clearly enough. It is a society in which the individual identifies his welfare with the welfare of the group, in which personal rights are subordinated to the rights of the group, and in which the individual expects to share his good fortune and in turn expects others to protect him from bad fortune. In sociological terms, the African is not "inner directed" but "other directed." His outlook, in politico-economic terms, is "communalized" or "socialized."

The "sentiments associated with *we*" have been the cement of African traditional society. In the new countries, perhaps the hardest task of leadership will be to expand the meaning of *we* from the tribe to the level of the nation.

NOMADIC HUNTERS, a family of Bushmen assembles by a tree in their arid Bechuanaland refuge. Only the family's matchless skill in hunting keeps its members alive.

The Living Forms of the Human Past

The entire sweep of human evolution is portrayed in modern Africa. The Stone Age has its counterpart in the wandering Bushmen. The dawn of settled agricultural life can be seen in thousands of tribe-dominated rural villages. Ancient Egypt's god-kings and medieval feudalism have their replicas here. So too does the modern dynamism of cities, factories and nation-states. But in time, Africa's new life will obliterate its older forms of human enterprise.

RURAL YOUNGSTER welcomes the cool drenching rain on a muddy street in his village (*left*), where he is protected by his tribe, his ancestors and the local gods.

VILLAGE MENFOLK lounge outside the cone-roofed huts of their compound, a fenced-in portion of a Nigerian village inhabited by several households linked by ties of kinship. The vast majority of Africans live in villages like this one and subsist on the maize, yams and other food crops they cultivate in small garden patches.

TRIBAL RITES help to maintain the fundamental bonds of loyalty to the group

COURT BALLET of Watutsi dancers performs for a chief, who sponsors them as a mark of prestige. The Watutsi, whose average height is more than six feet, were for centuries the overlords of Ruanda-Urundi. A leisure caste supported by their subjects, they dedicated themselves to dancing, high jumping and their beloved cattle.

CITY LIFE is infused with buoyant optimism in the newly independent nations

BUSTLING PEDESTRIANS enliven the streets of Kumasi (*above*), a commercial city which is also the tribal capital of Ghana's Ashanti folk.

TEEMING MARKET in Kumasi draws customers from all over Ghana (*opposite*) for brisk trading in anything from canned goods to fetishes.

ENTERPRISING PROMOTER in Kumasi sells fresh milk (*right*), a beverage that was almost totally lacking in the traditional Ghanaian diet.

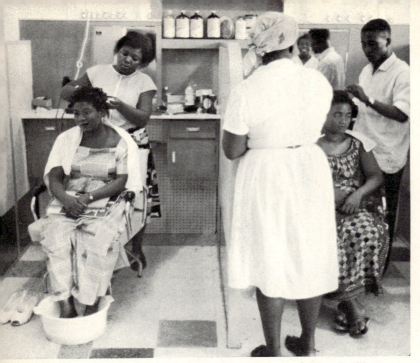

IN A BEAUTY PARLOR, a woman of Accra in Ghana gets her hair set and her feet treated. A full range of modern amenities can be found in Africa's thriving metropolises.

IN A SUPERMARKET in the Ivory Coast city of Abidjan, a girl loads an American-style shopping cart. The store is part of a chain found all over French-speaking Africa.

AT A FASHION SHOW in Accra, a model takes the customary stroll down the aisle. In Africa, only an elite minority can thus far afford the growing number of luxuries.

IN THE STACKS of the University College library in Ibadan (*opposite*), a Nigerian studies one of the library's 150,000 books, the largest collection in Tropical Africa.

Much as their ancestors did centuries ago, Bushmen migrate with all they possess in search of new hunting grounds. Driven south by more

powerful tribes, the Bushmen took refuge in the Kalahari Desert.

3

Migrations in the Mists of Time

ALL these mixtures of peoples, these count-less tribes with their private languages and customs—where did they come from, how did they arrive, how can they be accounted for? With all their dizzying variety they are, after all, cut from the same human material and share the emotions common to all mankind. What loves, hates and ambitions lie buried under the jungle floor and the grasslands of the endless savannas?

Most of Tropical Africa's past is not known. Most of it never can be, for except in recent times little of it was recorded. Amid the great babble of tongues, only a few African peoples ever developed any form of writing. For that matter, with similarly few exceptions, they did not develop any kind of calendar, so that even if there had been a way of writing about an event there would have been no way to put a date to it that would be intelligible to posterity. Thus for Tropical Africa there can never be an equivalent to the Rosetta Stone or the Aztec

Migrations in the Mists of Time

Calendar, no key whose discovery will unlock the riddle. In almost every aspect of early African history one can go just so far; then there is a blank door, and beyond it lies mystery.

Nevertheless, some things are known. Archaeologists and anthropologists and their scientific allies are, of course, used to working with bits and pieces and reconstructing a whole creature, society or epoch. Since, in Africa's case, the factual fragments are so much smaller than usual, the scientists are extremely cautious about giving answers, and they leave a great deal more in the realm of hypothesis. Consequently most of the statements that follow are opinions and hypotheses rather than assertions of fact.

The chances are that humanity—the *homo sapiens* that we all are, black, brown, yellow or pink—began in Africa, rather than in Asia as had long been thought. Such is the inference from anthropological discoveries made by the Leakeys—Dr. Louis S. B. Leakey, the Kenya-born British anthropologist, and his wife and co-worker, Mary—in the Olduvai Gorge of northern Tanganyika. In 1959 they found the skull and the tools of a primitive man 1,750,000 years old. Then in 1961 at Fort Ternan, in Kenya, they discovered a manlike creature that lived 14 million years ago. That Negroes, in particular, may be indigenous to Africa is not likely to cause general surprise; nevertheless, this theory runs contrary to an earlier one, which still has its scientific backers, that their homeland was some place in southern Asia and from there they migrated to Africa across the Suez land bridge, perhaps only some 8,000 or 9,000 years ago.

BE this as it may, as of several thousand years ago—perhaps as far back as 5000 B.C.—the African continent already was inhabited by the four major categories of human beings noted in the preceding chapter. There were people who were more or less like Pygmies, and others who resembled the Bushmen. There were Negroes. No one can say exactly what they looked like; probably there were many local variations. There were also those Caucasoid peoples—various and sundry, to whom various and sundry subdivisional classificatory labels have been attached—who lived in the north and east, spoke languages of the "Hamitic" group, and often have been referred to collectively as "the Hamites," a term of convenience we will also employ here. The pre-European history of Tropical Africa, that is to say up until the 15th Century, is largely concerned with the relationships among these peoples and, increasingly from the Seventh Century on, the Caucasoids who came from Arabia.

ONE of the foremost, if least known, developments of world history was the migrations of the Bantu-speaking Negroes. Their original homeland in Africa seems to have been Cameroon Mountain and its environs, where the Hump ends and the Atlantic coast line heads toward the south. Indeed, anthropologist G. P. Murdock asserts that, "On linguistic grounds it is impossible that the Bantu can have come from anywhere else." Almost nothing is known about their early history, but evidence suggests that some time near the First Century A.D. they began pushing outward from this region, expanding in eddies and waves until by about A.D. 500 they had taken over most of the Congo basin, which had been predominantly Pygmy. In the next few hundred years they spread on into east Africa, where they displaced or absorbed the Bushmen. From there they penetrated in massive numbers into southern Africa. The whole thing is as astonishing as it is inexplicable. As Murdock says, "The Bantu have revealed a capacity for explosive expansion paralleled, among all the other peoples of the world since the dawn of recorded history, only by the Arabs after Mohammed, the Chinese and the European nations since the Discoveries Period."

Meanwhile, some of the so-called Hamites had also begun moving, mainly toward the south, fanning out from three principal areas.

One of these was the high plateau, the highest and in some ways the most beautiful and habitable region of the whole continent, that comprises the western part of the present country of Ethiopia. From this lofty base and from Somalia—as nearly as events can be reconstructed—they spread into the great lakes region of Uganda and Ruanda-Urundi and into northern Kenya; probably south along the Indian Ocean coast as far as Zanzibar; south through Tanganyika, Northern Rhodesia and Nyasaland and possibly still farther to a place called Zimbabwe in present Southern Rhodesia; and conceivably even into parts of what is today the Republic of South Africa.

All of this occurred sporadically, erratically, planlessly and over a great period of time. In some instances the migrants encountered only Bushmen and Pygmies, whom they drove away or split into small, isolated pockets where their remnants can still be found. However, since the major migrations took place in the same era as those of the Bantu, the two rolling tides of humanity met: sometimes to live together peacefully, but often, it must be assumed, to dispute possession of the land in bloody raids and battles.

The second area from which Hamitic expansion took place was Egypt. From their homeland in the fertile delta and riverbanks of the lower part of the Nile, the ancient Egyptians expanded southward up the river to the middle region, encountering indigenous Negroes there. By 1580 B.C. they had occupied a considerable part of this region and had incorporated it into Upper Egypt. The Negroes acquired an infusion of Hamitic traits which in the course of time apparently were transmitted still farther up the river and eventually reached all the way to the shores of Lake Victoria.

FINALLY, the third general area from which Hamitic expansion took place was the northern coastal area of the continent, the fertile Mediterranean rim stretching from Egypt to the Atlantic and occupied today by Libya, Tunisia, Algeria and Morocco. The people indigenous there were a light-skinned (sometimes even blue-eyed and blond) group known as Berbers. Although they lie outside our area of

inquiry, they affected it in important ways—ways which merit further discussion later on but need to be indicated here.

In Chapter 1 it was noted that the natural impediment of the Sahara has tended to keep North Africa more or less separate from the rest of the continent. In ancient times this had not been so, for what is now desert was a lush green land teeming with life. Some thousands of years B.C. there still was rainfall enough to support widespread agriculture, and trade developed in the area—trade with both the peoples of the Mediterranean coast and those to the south, the goods carried by human porters along numerous well-trod trails. (Eventually their bare feet polished smooth the bedrock where the trails crossed rocky outcroppings.)

AS the climate became progressively drier, agriculture and trade withered, until by 2000 B.C. the great desert had formed. Yet life went on, though much restricted. Even the Saharan average of less than eight inches of rainfall a year allows some scanty seasonal vegetation, enough to support pastoral tribes and their flocks. Moreover, there are underground water supplies which here and there form natural oases and which can sometimes also be tapped by digging wells, and at such places there are sedentary agricultural communities. Trade continued, too, passing over some of the ancient trails. With the introduction of the camel (native to Asia) in A.D. 300, much bigger cargoes could be carried with greater ease and efficiency than was possible with the gangs of human bearers, and the trans-Saharan trade greatly increased. Eventually it grew huge, with camel trains sometimes numbering many thousands of animals accompanied by attendants, guards and merchants.

But in spite of the trails and oases, the Sahara was an uncomfortable, rugged and often dangerous place for travel. One may well wonder what enticements could have rewarded such a difficult journey. The trans-Saharan trade was based mainly on three precious commodities—salt, gold and slaves—which could be exchanged at great profit. The sequence of the commerce went as follows:

Berber trading parties from the north, with grain from their own area and with glassware, weapons and other articles from the Mediterranean countries, made their way through the Saharan settlements. They exchanged some of their goods for local produce such as dates and hides but loaded their main cargo, rock salt, at the desert's great deposits near Taghaza, Taotek and Taodeni. From here they continued into the Sudan.

DURING the European colonial era this word "Sudan" became identified with two distinct chunks of territory; the upper Nile valley and environs, known as the Anglo-Egyptian Sudan, and a big area on the western Hump that was called the French Sudan (now Mali); but properly it applies to the whole vast space of steppe and savanna that lies between the Sahara and the forest lands farther to the south, an area that stretches from the Atlantic at Dakar all the way across Africa to the Red Sea and is as much as a thousand miles from north to south. It is an Arab term, meaning "the Country of the Blacks," or simply "Negroland."

Here salt is rare. And it is even more rare and precious among the forest Negroes with whom the Sudanic peoples had always carried on trade. Toward the south, however, there were rich gold deposits, enabling the development of a natural commerce, a perfect example of the law of supply and demand. The Berbers bartered their salt and luxury goods to the Sudanese who, from their own domain and from their commerce with the south, could supply gold—as well as slaves, ivory, ebony, kola nuts and ostrich feathers—to be brought back up to the Mediterranean coast.

For some centuries this mutually profitable trade was carried on in comparative peace. The northern Berbers, mainly a sedentary agricultural people with a well-developed political democracy, had no expansionist ambitions. Their merchants had neither the inclination nor any practical motive for trying to conquer their Negro customers in the Sudan. There were, to be sure, some Berber pastoralist tribes which, in the search for more grazing lands, sometimes raided into the Sudan, but they seldom stayed long. In the Seventh Century A.D., however, the situation began to change when Arab invaders, inspired by the new faith of Mohammedanism, erupted into north Africa. They conquered Egypt, and then began a series of forays into Berber territories, where they soon became politically and economically powerful. Through generations of indoctrination by Arabs, many of the Berber upper classes and merchants became devout Moslems and were "Arabized" in many other ways. In the 11th and 12th Centuries, there was a new and much bigger eruption from Arabia—this time by illiterate and culturally backward nomads called Bedouins. They conquered the Berber states, despoiling and wrecking as they went along, and reducing many of the inhabitants to serfdom. This double-barreled Arabic intrusion had a marked effect in the lands to the south.

Islam is a militant faith. Even before the Bedouin influx, the Berbers had proselytized in the southern lands and had launched occasional invasions there, though these had been small-scale. The Bedouin invasions caused many Berbers to flee south into the Sahara, where they dispossessed or subjugated the Negroes who lived in the oases, and whence eventually some emerged into and occupied parts of the Sudan.

THEY brought with them, of course, their aggressive Islamic faith and their still more or less Arabized customs. Many of those who remained in the north were swept by a revivalist spirit which inspired them to launch *jihads* (holy wars) to conquer and convert the pagan peoples of the Sudan. Those of the northwestern Sudan, the first to absorb the new faith, spread it among their neighbors, who in turn passed it on, more often than not by force, so that eventually most of the peoples of the Sudan had become Moslems.

Thus, over a period of time, these northern Hamites (and the Arabs with whom they had

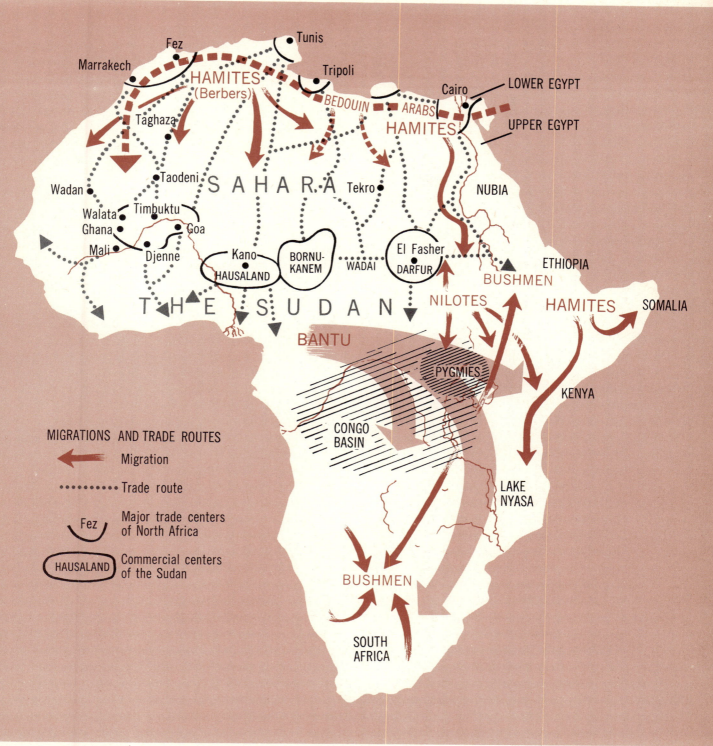

MIGRATIONS AND TRADE ROUTES

⬅ Migration

• • • • • • • • • • Trade route

⌣ Fez   Major trade centers of North Africa

(HAUSALAND)   Commercial centers of the Sudan

THE MOVEMENTS OF PEOPLES in Africa over many centuries are outlined above. Migrations would often result in one group intermingling with another or bringing the other under its control. Trade across the Sahara would be carried by camel as far south as the commercial centers of the Sudan, then on foot toward the coastal areas.

49

a variety of relationships) attained more and more influence in the Negro regions to the south. Through commerce, through political domination, and increasingly through settlement and ethnic merger they transmitted their civilization into Negro Africa.

These migratory currents and crosscurrents left their mark on African life in a variety of ways, all interrelated, but best understood if they are summarized separately.

FIRST, although biological adaptation probably accounts for many of the physical variations among the peoples of Africa, ethnic mixing is also an important factor. As noted in Chapter 2, only 35,000 to 40,000 "typical" Pygmies remain; most so-called Pygmies show evidences, in increased height or other features, of genetic admixture from other sources and have become, in anthropological parlance, "pygmoid"—meaning that they more or less resemble Pygmies. On the other hand, there are Pygmy and Bushman traces among many African peoples. A great amount of mixing also occurred between the Caucasoids and the Negroes. Whether the Caucasoids arrived in Negro regions as merchants, missionaries, settlers or as conquerors, whether they came from Ethiopia, the Nile valley or the Mediterranean area, they soon were intermarrying with the Negroes and in the long run tended to be absorbed by them. And because the Negroes were a constant source of slaves and concubines for the peoples to the north, there was a gradual absorption of Negro genetic traits among those who remained in the Caucasoid homelands. Today, as a result of migrations and this ethnic mixing all social strata in the Ethiopian highlands, for example, include a Negroid strain.

The outcome is a rich racial tapestry containing some fascinating oddities. There are the Somalis of the Horn, with interesting admixtures of Negro, Hamite, Arab and (Heaven knows) possibly Bushman, Phoenician, and East Indian ethnic qualities. There are the "Black Jews," the Falasha of Ethiopia, a Hamite-Negro mixture whose early ancestors were converted to Judaism and who in most instances live apart in self-chosen ghetto villages.

Particularly remarkable are the Fulani, an example of ethnic co-operation that began (according to Professor Murdock's account) in Senegal when Berber invaders were stopped by the strong Negro tribal state of the Tukulor. Since neither side could overcome the other, they apparently decided to live together. The Berbers accepted the language of the Negroes, and the Negroes accepted Islam, the religion of the Berbers. Soon they began to multiply and migrate; not, however, in large masses as the Bantu had done, but infiltrating and settling among other peoples, establishing enclaves and communities of their own. Today they can be found all over the western Sudan, from Senegal to Chad, and number at least six million: thoroughly mixed, but still often identifiable as predominantly Negroid or Caucasoid.

ONE of the major infiltrations of the Fulani occurred among the Hausas of Northern Nigeria, whose leaders, although professing Islam, eventually became laggard in their faith. In the early 19th Century, a Fulani holy man named Othman dan Fodio rallied the Fulani Faithful, declared a *jihad,* conquered the Hausa states, and deposited his chief lieutenants as ruling emirs under his central authority as Commander of the Faithful, which he exercised from the city of Sokoto. These emirates still exist, and their powerful political leader and spokesman is Othman dan Fodio's great-grandson, an intelligent, huge, quite dark-skinned man whose title is the Sardauna of Sokoto. Although the Hausa, now devout Moslems, have regained general equality, it is still the Fulani aristocracy who run the Nigerian north, and the Sardauna is its Premier. Since the north is more populous than the rest of Nigeria put together, the Fulani have a decisive voice in the affairs of this most important and most heavily populated nation of Tropical Africa. Quite certainly, if he had so wished, the Sardauna of Sokoto could have been Nigeria's first Prime Minister.

A second effect of the migrations was that in a good many cases migratory peoples established themselves as the aristocracy of the lands they entered. In such situations ethnic distinctions tended to become social distinctions, and some of these survived into modern times and became a source of social tensions—all too often encouraged by Europeans who saw in them a way to "divide and rule." Perhaps the most striking example has been that of Ruanda.

There, some centuries ago, the local Bantu inhabitants, a people known as the Hutu, had been invaded by the tall Nilotic Watutsi. Although vastly outnumbered by the Hutu, the Watutsi gradually subjugated them and settled down to a life of privilege: they became an upper-crust caste of warriors, property owners, languid aristocrats who kept the Hutu in near-serfdom and "cleverly exploited" (in the words of one respected scholar, Professor J. J. Maquet) ". . . their slender figure and their light skin in order to affirm the idea of a natural superiority over the Hutu, who are of ordinary stature and with coarse features."

The situation was reinforced during the European colonial era. Under Germany, which had acquired Ruanda as part of its "zone of influence" in Africa, and much more under Belgium, which ran the country for the League of Nations after World War I and later for the U.N., the Watutsi were deferred to, supported and used—used as the instrument by which the Europeans could indirectly rule the country. They were the ones who received education. They became the administrators. Their power grew; so did their pride and arrogance.

NEVERTHELESS, inevitably if slowly, literacy and enlightenment finally began to spread among the Hutu—and so did their demands for a more democratic distribution of political and economic benefits. By the late 1950s the Belgians, belatedly realizing that the future in Africa belonged to the masses rather than the classes, were encouraging Hutu aspirations. The Watutsi remained arrogantly self-assured and uncompromising. Late in 1959 the scene exploded when the Hutu rebelled amid horrendous scenes of fire, pillage and bloodshed. In 1961 they deposed the Watutsi king; and later that year, taking no chances on a Watutsi revival, repeated the fire and pillage before a U.N.-sponsored election which was supposed to create a fully representative government.

In neighboring Urundi, which is ethnically similar and has the same general history of German and Belgian occupation, events turned out differently. Here—possibly because of more intermarriage between the Hutu and Watutsi—the physical differences between the two peoples are less marked, and class distinctions and antagonisms have been less acute. The king was widely thought of as a stabilizing influence. So there was no revolution: in fact, in the 1961 U.N. election the party that was more identified with the king and aristocracy won. But the harmony is relative and may still prove temporary. For wherever social distinctions reflect ethnic differences (as is still considerably the case in Urundi) social peace is precarious. A list of the other stress points would include Ethiopia, Uganda, the Republic of Sudan and Zanzibar—to name a few.

A THIRD important aspect of ethnic intermingling is its effect on Africa's food. For the European and the American it takes effort to think of food in terms of survival. But in a subsistence economy such as prevailed in most of Tropical Africa, getting enough to eat is a central concern of life, and this has been reflected in African religious beliefs, art, customs and, of course, political behavior.

Here, as is so often the case in Africa, we confront a seeming paradox. Consider the rain forests such as Winston Churchill described: a hundred plants counted at random would include 30 or 40 species. The forests of the Ivory Coast contain at least 500 species of trees including 248 different genera and 55 different families. And these plants support an equally various insect, reptile and animal life. Look at the savanna, the habitat of Africa's famous wild game: the marvelous and beautiful varieties of antelope, the elephants, zebras, giraffes, gnus and other herbivores which in turn support the carnivores, the cheetahs, leopards and lions.

For that matter, among the flocks and gardens and farms of contemporary Africa one can find some 90 per cent of all the cultivated plants of the world and most of the domesticated animals: camels, cattle, sheep, goats, horses, mules, donkeys, dogs, cats, chickens and other useful fowl. All of this seems so much a part of the natural order—goats frisking in the villages, banana and coconut trees sheltering the thatch huts—that one might assume it has always been that way. And yet, except for the wild life, and perhaps the larger part of the forest growths, little of it is indigenous to Africa.

AMONG the domesticated creatures only the dog, the guinea fowl and possibly the donkey, and among foods only oil palm, millet, eleusine, sorghum (Guinea corn) and a few others, are native. All the rest came from somewhere else, a few (like maize and manioc) from the New World, but most from Asia. They were secured—in ways lost to history—through migrants from Arabia, India and Indonesia, and by the Berbers, the ancient Egyptians and the Hamites of the Horn and eastern coast, all of whom had commerce with the peoples of the East where agriculture and civilization began.

The acquisition of these useful plants and animals had a decisive effect on both the Bantu and the Hamitic migrations, and consequently on much that has happened in Africa since. Why the Bantu first began to move, no one can know. Apparently what enabled them to move, however, was that they possessed some of these "new" basic food plants, especially the yam, banana and the taro (an edible root)—and thus they could eat, survive and multiply. They continued to move because they multiplied, and because the African soil is generally thin and poor and is soon worn out from successive plantings; and because of a strange technological hiatus: they never discovered the plow.

This implement was, of course, known and used by the ancient Egyptians, and it was in use in most of the Hamitic regions by the time the Bantu migrations began. But for inexplicable reasons the idea did not spread into Bantu areas. The Bantu used a primitive form of hoe for cultivation; and to enrich the soil they burned the covering forest or other vegetation. With these methods they were forced by their natural increase to reach out for new lands.

The Hamites, too, had to contend with soil and geography. In their homelands they could raise both food crops and livestock, but as they expanded along routes that we have traced into regions where rainfall was too scanty or too undependable for crops, they had to rely increasingly on their herds. Necessity developed into a virtue; animal husbandry became endowed with patriotic and mystical qualities, requiring that the herds grow ever larger and more and more grazing land be found for them.

Time has brought cultural as well as ethnic interchange, so that now one finds Bantu and other Negro peoples who practice herding, peoples of Hamitic language or culture traits who practice agriculture, and tribes that combine both. Nevertheless, in large parts of Tropical Africa, the rivalry between the crop cultivators and the pastoralists still persists. Even where the feud has ended, it has left its residue in traditions that shape the behavior and mental outlook of many Africans and create problems.

THE ownership of herd animals became a badge of superiority and a symbol of wealth. Cattle became, in fact, a kind of living currency, a store of riches and a medium of exchange. In Kenya when Tom Mboya, one of the best known African nationalist leaders, married Pamela Odede, a recent graduate of Western College in Ohio, he promised to pay a "bride price" of 16 cows. "This price would have been 12 if I had been kind, or 24 if I had been harsh," commented the bride's father, Walter Odede, who also is active in Kenya politics (he spent some years in "detainment" as a suspected Mau Mau leader). "That is what a daughter is worth according to custom. The cows will be paid in installments."

Prim-looking giraffes browse on a grassy rise not far from Mount Kilimanjaro, a perennially snow-capped volcano 19,340 feet high.

The Forceful Drama of Massive Forms

A raised platform of rigid rock, the African continent seems made to provoke the restless migrations of men. For thousands of square miles under a wide-open sky, the land rolls so gently and tediously that it appears to offer no perch for settlement. But set against that provoking monotony is the massive drama of thrusting volcanoes, tangled rain forests and craggy escarpments cut by rain-swollen rivers—the outsize features of a land built on a titanic scale.

MIGHTY FALLS cut into the massive continental plateau as rivers eat their way to the low-lying coast

TOWERING SPRAY rises high over Victoria Falls as the Zambezi River drops hundreds of feet into Boiling Pot gorge. Discovered in 1855 by David Livingstone and known to Africans as the "Smoke That Thunders," Victoria Falls sets up a roar heard 10 miles away. Its spray, falling over a wide area like a never-ending rainstorm, waters an exuberant stand of jungle. A 650-foot-long bridge completed in 1904 spans the deep gorge.

VACANT GRASSLAND in the east African plains is dotted with thorn trees whose flat tops are well adapted to catch the maximum moisture during the scanty rainy season.

LACY GROVE of fern-covered palm trees in the towering coastal jungle of Nigeria (*opposite*) is slowly crossed by a tribesman carrying a load of oil-yielding palm fruit.

WILLIFE once

thrived on the plains

in unparalleled numbers

and variety, but today

the animal population

is rapidly dying out

TWILIGHT RUN of a troop of zebras kicks up dust on a game preserve near Nairobi, Kenya. Fifty years ago, uncountable millions of wild animals wheeled about freely throughout the grasslands of East Africa. Since then, savaged by hunters and pushed out by cattle raisers, 90 per cent of the wildlife has been destroyed. The rest are now protected by stringent law in national parks, but relentless poaching is killing off even this remnant.

GLINTING SURFACE of the Congo (*above*) is cut by a slender river craft near Stanleyville. At this point, 1,300 miles upstream, the jungle river is about 10 miles wide.

FROTHY CASCADE of water churns between rocks at Murchison Falls (*opposite*), where a branch of the Nile funnels through a series of clefts as narrow as 19 feet.

4

Fabled Kingdoms of Antiquity

UNTIL the past few hectic years, when most Europeans and Americans thought about Africa—to the extent that they thought about it at all—the terms of reference were marvelously simple. They consisted of what the white man was doing there. He was a big game hunter, or he was a missionary, or an explorer, or a mining engineer, or a colonial administrator; he was "developing Africa," "opening it up." Africa itself was something large, dark and supine, and the African people were an amorphous and primitive mass. They were people for whom there would be a future, thanks to the efforts of the white man, but as far as the

Europeans and Americans knew, they had no past. As Lord Milverton, a former Governor of Nigeria, wrote in 1952: "For countless centuries, while all the pageant of history swept by, the African remained unmoved—in primitive savagery."

The terms have changed now: attention is riveted on what the black man is doing. But what is still not generally realized is that he had been making his own history, in his own ways, for a very long time. The drama in its earliest phase was unknown to Europe and America because no Europeans or Americans were there to witness it; but it was nevertheless being played, the cast was immense and the action vivid.

The Arab historian al-Bakri wrote this description 900 years ago: "The King of Ghana can put 200,000 warriors in the field, more than 40,000 being armed with bow and arrow. . . . When he gives audience to his people . . . he sits in a pavilion around which stand his horses caparisoned in cloth of gold; behind him stand 10 pages holding shields and gold-mounted swords; and on his right hand are the sons of the princes of his empire, splendidly clad and with gold plaited into their hair."

WHERE was Ghana; what happened to it? Where are the kings and princes, and where is the gold?

This kingdom of history and, even more, of legend lay in the far western Sudan, taking in the headwaters of the Senegal and Niger Rivers, and probably was much larger than modern France. Its capital, a city of perhaps 30,000, lay in the southeast corner of the present country of Mauritania. The city has vanished long ago. But it must have been a bustling, colorful place, for it was the western terminus of the Taodeni Trail, the main caravan route that led south from Morocco through the Sahara's most important salt deposits to the sources of gold. And even allowing for some imagination and exaggeration (al-Bakri reported also that the king owned a gold nugget so big he tethered his horse to it), the royal government must have been an impressive enterprise. The king, a sacred personage, presided over a hierarchy of nobles, chiefs and subchiefs who carried out his orders, collected taxes and customs duties, and monopolized on his behalf all the gold that was found or imported into the kingdom.

What happened to Ghana was the same thing that happened, in one version or another, in later times in many parts of the western Sudan and its adjoining forest areas. In 1076, after a long campaign, a Berber army of "Almoravids" —a puritanical, crusading Islamic sect—captured Ghana's capital. In the words of another Arab historian, Ibn Khaldun, the Almoravid Berbers "spread their dominion over the Ne-groes, devastated their territory and plundered their property. Having submitted them to poll tax they imposed on them a tribute, and compelled a great number of them to become Moslems. . . . [Later] their neighbors, the Sosso, took their country and reduced its inhabitants to slavery."

Nearly nine centuries later, in 1957, a new state of Ghana came into being when the British Gold Coast colony secured independence. Actually the Gold Coast lay far to the south of old Ghana and the people are a different group of Negroes with a different history and language. Nevertheless Kwame Nkrumah and his colleagues, whose nostalgia for Africa's past glories has been exceeded only by their ambitions for the future, appropriated the name of the old kingdom. The Gold Coast vanished, and Ghana reappeared on the map.

THE old Kingdom of Ghana was not the only example of the African's ability to organize and operate large units of government. There were at least a few before it and there were a great many afterward. Indeed, although with weaker authority and in somewhat vestigial form, more than 40 of them—"states" ranging in size from a few thousand people to hundreds of thousands—still survive as part of the governing apparatus of the new nations or of what remains of the European colonial system. There is no need to catalogue them all. Some, however, deserve special notice because of the way they illuminate the past and, in a rather surprising number of instances, connect it directly with the present.

Much as it fills today's headlines, "African nationalism" was a topical issue in the Nile valley around 800 B.C. By that time the Nubians, who were conquered by the Egyptians around 2000 B.C., had acquired such military and technical proficiency that they were able to force their conquerors to grant them independence. Not long afterward they reversed the current of a thousand years by invading and subduing Egypt and establishing their kings on the throne of the Pharaohs, making up Egypt's

25th Dynasty. Within a few generations the Nubians were driven out of Egypt by the Assyrians, but in their own territories, known as the Kingdom of Kush, they remained sovereign and strong until disaster overtook them around A.D. 300. Kush, in other words, existed as an independent nation for more than a thousand years.

TO this day the relations of this area vis-à-vis Egypt have never been stabilized for long. In the early 19th Century, after innumerable vicissitudes, it again came fully under Egyptian rule, which subsequently was shared by the British in an arrangement known as a "condominium." From then until 1956 it was part of the "Anglo-Egyptian Sudan," a vast space, more than four times the size of Texas, that stretched west into the Sahara and south all the way to Uganda. It took in numerous primitive peoples, mainly Negroid, including the naked Tumtums and those formidable and dignified Nilotes, the Dinka, the Nuer and the Shilluk. The British held the polyglot creation together, however, and in 1953 gave it self-government for a transitional period, with the right to decide later whether it preferred to unite with Egypt or become fully independent. The Sudanese parliament chose the latter and set up the present Republic of Sudan, to the chagrin of the Egyptians, who have been busy ever since —with economic pressures, military threats and all the devices of boring from within—trying to undo the result and bring about the union; a union which they would dominate.

In neighboring Ethiopia, the past in many ways *is* the present. This big and potentially important country—with 18 million people in an area four times the size of the state of Wyoming—has been almost a living fossil, immobilized and isolated by its history and, perhaps quite as much, by its legends. Of all the Ethiopian traditions, none is more vividly alive and pertinent than the familiar story of the Queen of Sheba—how she heard of the fame of Solomon and "came," as the Bible relates, "to prove him with hard questions," bringing a train of camels laden with spices, gold and precious stones.

Ethiopians believe that the Queen of Sheba had her capital at Axum, in northeast Ethiopia, and that after she returned she bore a son by Solomon, named him Menelik and gave the throne to him when he grew to manhood. According to Ethiopian history, this was the beginning of the "Solomonic Dynasty," whose present representative is His Imperial Majesty Haile Selassie, Emperor of Ethiopia, King of Kings, Elect of God and (by descent from Solomon) Conquering Lion of Judah. Through marriages between members of the royal family and Ethiopian nobility during the millennia, most upper-class Ethiopians today are able to trace their ancestry back to Menelik and the romance of Solomon and Sheba.

OBJECTIVE historians think that the Biblical Queen of Sheba came not from Ethiopia but from Saba, a thriving country across the Red Sea where Yemen and Aden now are located, and that not until many years after her death did the Sabaeans, an aggressive, technically advanced people, cross over into Ethiopia. They subdued the local Hamites, seized the northern part of Ethiopia and eventually created there the powerful kingdom known as Axum. It was Axum that demolished the Kingdom of Kush around A.D. 300. It was the Axumites who also brought Christianity to Ethiopia, having themselves been converted to that faith in the Fourth Century A.D. In the isolation of their highland redoubt, ". . . the Aethiopians," as the British historian Edward Gibbon recorded metaphorically, "slept near a thousand years, forgetful of the world, by whom they were forgotten." While Islam eddied around them, they retained their Christian faith, and today Ethiopia is the only African country with a strong Christian tradition.

Despite the considerable doubt that historians have cast upon the Ethiopian version of the Queen of Sheba's visit to Solomon, the story has the status of fact in Ethiopia. It was both a cause and a symbol of the archaic government and society with which Ethiopia entered the modern era. With a semidivine monarch; with an aristocracy of great landowning families whose members also filled all the important jobs in the government, army and church; with a vast, poverty-ridden, oppressed peasantry living in virtual serfdom in the highlands and, in the lower lands, a population of wild, Stone-Age tribes whom the government made little effort to civilize; with an officialdom steeped in corruption, ignorance and internecine plotting and fighting, Ethiopia was a weird combination of feudalism and savagery. And to a large extent it still is. In the years since World War II, when the interval of Italian conquest and occupation (1935 to 1941) ended and Haile Selassie was restored to the throne, there have been serious efforts to catch up with the world, particularly in education and transportation. But the pace is painfully slow, clogged every inch of the way by the inertia of the centuries; and Ethiopia—the oldest of the independent nations of Tropical Africa—remains among the most backward.

WHILE "the Aethiopians slept," history was swirling around their citadel; in every direction kingdoms rose and fell, and new languages, peoples and social structures were created. Saba vanished, but its descendants, Moslem Yemenites, continued trading down the east African coast. Mixing there with the Bantu peoples and others, they left their legacy in a polyglot dark-skinned but Arabized coastal population and a hybrid language, Swahili (mainly Bantu with an infusion of Arabic words), that became the trading language of eastern and central Africa. Southwest of the Ethiopian plateau, Bantu, Nilotes, and migratory Hamites contended and combined in a kaleidoscopic pattern of tribal states and chiefdoms and kingdoms. Some of these survived into modern times, notably the kingdom of the Shilluks, the twin kingdoms of Ruanda and Urundi, and the four kingdoms—Toro, Bunyoro, Ankole and Buganda—of the present country of Uganda.

Buganda attained one of the most stable and highly developed governments in Tropical Africa, with a parliament, a code of laws and courts of justice, an administrative bureaucracy, a hereditary nobility and a royal family whose lineage goes back some 400 years. Much of this apparatus, including the throne (occupied since 1942, except for a brief exile, by Edward William Frederick David Walugeme Mutebi Luwangula Mutesa, His Highness Mutesa II), continued in operation during the period of British colonial rule. Its strength, in fact, was the largest obstacle to Uganda's independence; for Buganda, proud of being the biggest, richest and most highly developed of the four kingdoms, was determined to dominate the government of an independent Uganda or to detach itself and go its own way. The ambitions still persist; they will disturb the politics of independent Uganda for a long time to come.

AMONG many similar connections between the old and the new and yet-to-be, there are a few other names that will be useful to know. We have seen how, in the far western region of the Sudan, Ghana rose and fell—and was "reborn" symbolically in another location. We have seen also that the Sudan is a vast region, great parts of which were subjected to the same kinds of influences through the trans-Saharan trade and Berber and Arab incursions. It was logical, therefore, that other states besides Ghana should arise there.

Perhaps the most important of them was Mali. Its rulers had been subordinate chiefs within Ghana's empire and were part of the same branch of the Negroes as Ghana's founders. After Ghana's fall, they expanded, gradually absorbing the fragments of the old empire and eventually reaching out to conquer a much larger territory. At its apogee in the 14th Century, Mali dominated most of the area of the upper and middle Niger River basin, a space roughly twice the size of California, and hence commanded the richest share of the gold and salt trade. Its king then, known as Kankan Musa, was a devout Moslem, his ancestors having been converted when the Almoravids invaded Ghana. He made a pilgrimage to Mecca accompanied by a retinue that included, according to the perhaps romanticized accounts of Arab writers, 500 slaves each carrying a golden staff and a camel train bearing tons of gold.

Within a few generations after Kankan Musa's death in 1332, Mali began disintegrating under the attack of warlike neighbors, and within a few more generations it was reduced to inconsequence and its fragments were digested by other rising states. But its legend remained. And in 1960, when the territories of French West Africa became independent, the one that had been known as the French Sudan became the Republic of Mali—with propriety, in this case, since most of the earlier Mali was actually contained in the area of the new nation. Modibo Keita, the republic's first president, traces his descent from a certain Sundiata Keita, one of the earliest kings of Mali.

Mali's successor as the leading power in the western Sudan was Songhai. Its name has yet to reappear on the modern map, but the name of its greatest king, Mohammed Askia, has an exalted place in the pantheon of African nationalism, for he left Negro Africa with a highly prized tradition of intellectual achievement.

HIS principal city was the fabled Timbuktu. Founded centuries earlier by the Songhai people, this place had become an alternate southern terminus for the Taodeni caravan trail and hence had grown into a rich and important center of trade. Mali's Kankan Musa, who possessed it for a while, had graced it with some mosques and thus started its cultural progress, but it remained for Mohammed Askia to make it a center of learning famous throughout the Islamic world. During his regime it acquired a university and became a remarkably advanced society. According to a writer of that day, "In Timbuktu there are numerous judges, doctors, and clerics, all receiving good salaries from the king. He pays great respect to men of learning."

Sixty-three years after Mohammed Askia's reign ended in 1528, all this and the Songhai empire as well suffered the same fate as Ghana:

REMOTE TIMBUKTU, which flourished 600 years ago, was sketched in 1828 by René Caillié, a Frenchman who was the first European to visit the city and report on it.

Moroccan armies arrived, conquered the country and looted the cities. When the first European explorers saw Timbuktu in the early part of the 19th Century, it had become just another unremarkable jumble of mud houses—which, sadly, is also true today.

Mohammed Askia took the Songhai throne in 1493; Timbuktu fell to the Moroccans in 1591. These dates, which span the period of highest development in the Sudan, have another special significance as well. For the 15th Century brought the opening of the Age of Discovery. Columbus's voyage to the New World had a fatal meaning for Tropical Africa in general, as we shall see, but in a particular way it led to a decline in the fortunes of the Sudan. Europeans, with a new daring and enthusiasm for exploration by sea, sailed around Africa's western Hump; they were followed by merchant adventurers, and soon there were trading posts scattered along the Hump's nether side, the Guinea Coast. The gold and the ivory and ebony and ostrich plumes and slaves, all those staples of the trans-Saharan traffic, began more and more to flow southward to the coast rather than northward to the Sudanic trading towns.

With the coming of the Age of Discovery and its daring new voyages around the Hump, the Sudan was outflanked. The process took time, and meanwhile substantial kingdoms—Wadai, Bagirmi, Kanem and Bornu—appeared there, but the future lay with the peoples of the forests and coastal regions, where a group of powerful kingdoms had begun to emerge. Yoruba and Benin, and later Dahomey and Ashanti—these were newly important names, but they belong to the period of European development which will be discussed in the next chapter.

TO round out our view of pre-European Africa we need to look farther south, toward the basin of the Congo; for here, again, today's political happenings are rooted in the past. When, in 1482, the first Portuguese explorers arrived at the mouth of the Congo River, they found a large and thriving kingdom. There was a capital city and a royal court, an aristocracy of governors, chiefs and functionaries, and an efficient system of tax collection.

A European traveler wrote this description: "The King of Congo, when hee goeth to the Campe to see his Armie, rideth upon an Elephant in great pompe and majestie, on either side of the Elephant he hath six slaves two of them were Kings, that he himselfe had taken in the field. . . . Then there followeth a More, which doth nothing but talke aloud in praise of the King, telling what a great Warriour he hath beene, and praising his wisdome for all things that hee hath accomplished. . . ." In 1491 the king was baptized a Christian, and thereafter he exchanged ambassadors with the Pope and the King of Portugal.

This Kingdom of the Kongo (the usual spelling) had declined and fallen by the mid-16th Century, but a remnant lived on. In the 19th Century an explorer found the last of the royal line, still calling himself King of the Kongo,

presiding in tattered pomp over an insignificant jungle village. In the 1950s a tribal association known as the Association of the Lower Congo —ABAKO, for short—grew up in the domain of the old kingdom; its aims, along with certain social and protective ones, included the "cultural reintegration" of the area and (though this was thought of, in those days, as the distant future) its political independence.

On the French side of the river, in the territory known then as Middle Congo, ABAKO's leader was a defrocked priest-turned-politician, *Abbé* Fulbert Youlou: he went on to become mayor of Brazzaville, the principal city, and not long afterward, when the French possessions became free nations, president of what he quickly renamed the Congo Republic. On the Belgian side ABAKO's head was a sometime teacher and politician named Joseph Kasavubu—who presided over ABAKO meetings from a throne decked out with leopard skins and other regal symbols. In 1960, when independence came to the Belgian Congo, Joseph Kasavubu moved into the former palace of the governor as the first chief of state of what also was renamed as the Republic of the Congo.

KASAVUBU'S well-known subsequent difficulties and those of the republic stem in part from the fact that the old Belgian Congo incorporated other substantial kingdoms. Their names are meaningless to the world at large, but significant in their time and significant now again in the legacies of pride and mutual suspicion they have left. There were the Bushongo people, for instance, with their great king-hero Shamba Bolongongo, whose exploits and wisdom are the subject of countless tales. The Luba people had a substantial empire in the 18th Century; later they became widely dispersed in the southeast parts of the Congo.

Most important—in the light of events—there was the Lunda empire. Its beginnings were in the 17th Century, when a warrior king called Mwata Yamvo set the Lunda tribe on a course of conquest that carried them to dominance over all the tribes of the central Congo.

The Lunda kings—who bore the title Mwata Yamvo in honor of the founder—were quite powerful when the Belgians arrived; and although their authority later was limited to tribal affairs, they continued to receive the respect of the Lunda and to maintain a royal court.

IN 1939 a young man named Moise Tshombe, son of a wealthy Lunda merchant, married the daughter of a Lunda chief who subsequently became king—Mwata Yamvo Ditende Yawa Nawezi III. Moise Tshombe got into politics in his home province of Katanga, where the Lunda are among the biggest of the numerous tribes. When the Belgians called provincial elections preparatory to granting Congolese independence, Tshombe, aided by his father-in-law's blessing and the support of his tribe, was elected president of the Katanga government—and from this position led the attempted secession of Katanga from the new republic.

The Congo's troubles have come from many sources: a more tangled skein would be hard to imagine. Later we will see some of the other components. But the point to be noted here is that the antagonisms and clashing ambitions that emerged so quickly were, in many cases, the modern residue of far older ones whose sources lay in the tribes and kingdoms.

That Africans have the capacity to create and maintain large-scale units of government, and had it a long time before the Europeans came on the scene, is obvious. Not only the modern African national leaders but the people who wish them well can take satisfaction in this fact.

However, the fact raises certain questions. What about our earlier observation (*Chapter 2*) that the tribe—and even more, its smaller components, the clan and village—has been the traditional social unit in African life? The earlier statement holds. Numerous though the kingdoms were, they were far from being typical; and powerful though the kings might be, their power usually rested on the subjugation of people whose loyalties and interests remained attached to their village and clan or, at the highest level, their own tribe. Except at the tribal level,

it was rare to find anything that fitted Webster's definition of a nation: "A people connected by supposed ties of blood generally manifested by community of language, religion and customs . . . ; any group of people having like institutions and customs and a sense of social homogeneity and mutual interest."

There is another important point to be made —important for what it may indicate about Africa's future political development. At the level of the village, the clan group and fairly often of the tribe, African government traditionally has a good many elements of democracy. Or, let us say, of a "democratic republic," since the universal franchise—the "one man, one vote" idea advanced so enthusiastically by today's African nationalists in places such as Kenya—has practically no precedent. But the "republican" idea that government should be in the hands of those best fitted to govern is widely prevalent in one form or another, usually in the form of a Council of Elders.

THESE older, wiser men not only advise the chief but often have the power of veto and even the right to depose him if he makes arbitrary decisions without having properly consulted them. Or, in tribes with well-defined "age sets" the chief, if there is one at all, may be only a kind of presiding officer, and decisions are made jointly and through open discussion by all the members of the governing "set," which consists of men of middle age or older.

This republican concept has tended to fade as the unit of government grows bigger and to be replaced by authoritarianism. At the level of the "nations" or "states" we have been discussing, the form of government is most often despotism. The king's power tends to become absolute, his decisions arbitrary, his person itself awesome and sacred. Not only does he rule by divine right: he is a divinity, like the Egyptian Pharaohs of old, and presides over a court that is not only a court but a shrine.

It remains to be seen how far this authoritarian tradition may influence the political destinies of Africa in its new age of nationalism.

The Durable Force of Regal Authority

Kings and chiefs are a living force in Africa, although their power now takes a variety of forms. There are independent kingdoms like Ethiopia where the authority of the emperor depends on his subjects' faith that he descends directly from the Biblical House of David. There are kingdoms harbored within larger nations like the Buganda of Uganda. There are leaders like Nigeria's Sardauna of Sokoto whose power takes the modern form of controlling a mass of votes. Behind the sophisticated paraphernalia of presidential elections and parliamentary maneuverings often lies the personal spiritual authority of descendants of ancient royal dynasties.

LIVE GOODS, sheep and goats are traded at a weekly market (*above*) in an upland Ethiopian village. The rugged terrain prevents large-scale transportation of goods.

FOREIGN IMPORT, a recently built cotton spinning mill in Ethiopia (*left*) is owned by Greeks and Armenians, who control and run many of the country's few factories.

CHRISTIAN WORSHIPERS congregate outside a church in Addis Ababa to await the emperor, titular head of the Ethiopian Orthodox Church. Most of Ethiopia's Christians are Amharas, the nation's ruling minority. The Amharas, who consider themselves "white," have been known to look on Europeans as an inferior "pink" race.

NOBLE ANCESTRY is a key

source of prestige in the contemporary

struggle for political power

REPUBLICAN ROYALTY, Modibo Keita (*above*), President of the Mali Republic, claims descent from a Mandingo chief who ruled the 13th Century empire of Mali.

HERO'S GRANDSON, Sékou Touré, President of Guinea, associates himself with the memory of Almany Samory Touré (seen in portrait), a near-legendary tribal warrior.

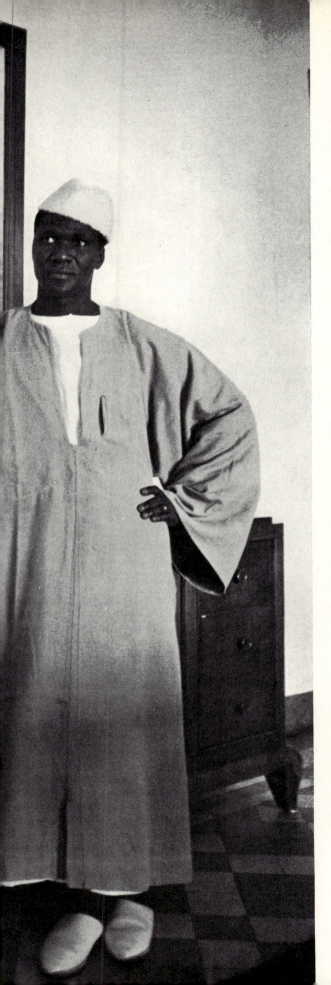

WATUTSI KING of Ruanda, Kigeri V, was given the throne in 1959 upon the sudden death of his half brother. He lost it in 1961 when the subject peoples revolted.

75

LONG LIVE THE KABAKA
KABAKA MUTESA II

*MAJESTY is personified
in a young sovereign
who holds sway over
a nation within a nation
now seeking its own
political independence*

RETURNING FROM EXILE, King Mutesa II of Buganda, a kingdom in
Uganda, is cheered in 1955 (*left*) as
he is driven through his realm. He
had been exiled by the British for op-
posing their plans for a federation.

IN HIS REGALIA, the King of Buganda
(*opposite*), Cambridge-educated, wears
a white satin hat and stands beneath a
tattered umbrella. The kingdom, with
more than one million subjects, has
been in existence for some 400 years.

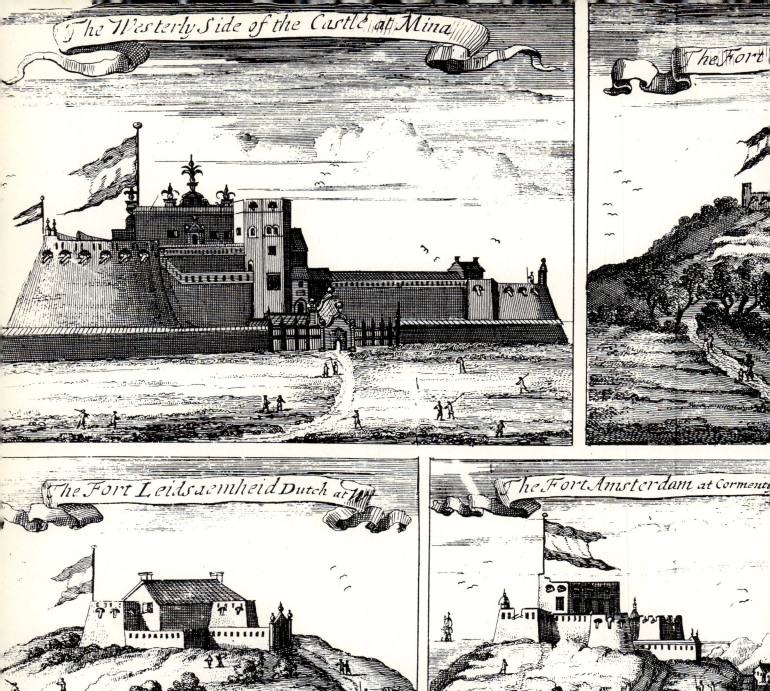

The Westerly Side of the Castle at Mina

The Fort

The Fort Leidsaemheid Dutch at W

The Fort Amsterdam at Cormentz

Fort Christiaansburgh at Acra at W

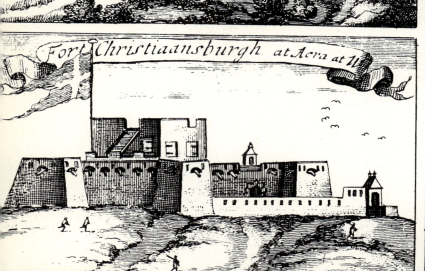

Fort Creveceur at Acra at

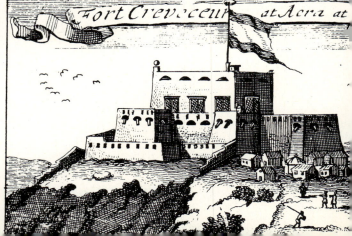

5

Exploitation on an Epic Scale

THE largest city in Tropical Africa is Ibadan, the capital of the Western Region of Nigeria. Its population is about 600,000. The largest urban aggregation of people of African descent, however, is not in Africa but in New York City: there, centered on Harlem, they number well over one million, almost twice the size of Ibadan. In the United States as a whole, about 10 per cent of the population descends from Africa: nearly 19 million people, a number far greater than the population of any Tropical African nation except Nigeria.

The figures have to be qualified at once, of course, by inserting the word "predominantly," because a large majority of Americans of dark skin, even though it may be very dark indeed, have at least some heritage of "white" blood. On the other hand a certain number of "white" Americans have some unacknowledged or unknown admixture of African blood. So the figure of 10 per cent is conservative.

There are at least as many people of African or mixed African ancestry in Brazil as in the U.S., and if we add those of Central America, the northern rim of South America and the islands of the Caribbean, it is likely that their number in the New World would be on the order of 50 to 60 million—about a third as big as the population of Tropical Africa itself.

But this is not the whole of the matter. In all the countries of the Mediterranean and the Middle East (particularly those of the Arabian peninsula), in Iran, in India and Ceylon, in the Malay peninsula, in the East Indies and even in China, there is an increment of African blood. Truly, the African is a world citizen.

THIS peculiar role was thrust upon the African; it was entirely involuntary. In fact it was the result of criminal immorality on such an enormous scale, over such a long time, involving so many guilty men so variously placed, that there is scarcely any crime that can be compared with it, perhaps not even the Nazi barbarities against the Jews.

What accounted for that monstrous institution, the African slave trade? Who were the men who were responsible for it? How did it affect Africa at the time—and now?

Among the numerous "theories of history" there is one, the materialist theory, which maintains that all major human events derive ultimately from economic causes. This, of course, is not true, and addiction to it leads to such perversities as the Marxist-Leninist brand of communism. In the particular case of the slave trade, however, materialism, if it does not supply all the answers, supplies something like 90 per cent of them. This may in turn have something to do with the materialistic ideas that modern African nationalist leaders often display in their foreign policies, which tend to be markedly unsentimental.

The trade in African slaves was not a foreign invention. In the first instance, of course, it was African—a generally characteristic part of the African tradition. Africans had captured and used or sold one another in all likelihood from earliest times, just as peoples in other parts of the world enslaved one another and as some continued to do until very recent times. Moreover, as we have seen, slaves were a standard article of commerce in the trans-Saharan trade which built the Sudanic kingdoms; and in those kingdoms, and practically all others of

which there is any record, the ownership of slaves was as routine a mark of affluence as the ownership of gold or any other valuable commodity. This enslavement of Africans by Africans persisted until European hegemony was established. Indeed, among some tribes it exists to this day in effect, if not in form. Slaves have been replaced by subservient groups of people, the descendants of slaves or serfs, who are bound to the ruling groups by the powerful force of tradition.

As for the shipping of slaves from Africa on an organized, commercial basis—the context one ordinarily associates with the slave trade—this goes back in rudimentary form at least to the Fifth Century B.C., the time when Carthage was flourishing, but its development can properly be assigned to the Arabs located in the Arabian peninsula. By the end of the Seventh Century A.D., at the latest, and with interruptions until well into the 19th Century, the Arabs dominated the east African coastal trade, carrying away—with other typical commodities of the region—masses of slaves to Arabia, where some were sold for local use and others were dispersed through trade channels to distant buyers. Some of them were shipped to India and the islands beyond, and at least a few went all the way to China.

WITH their invasions of North Africa the Arabs fastened their grip on the trans-Saharan slave traffic. Infiltrating the continent both from the east and the north, they organized the trade at its sources of supply, the tribes of the hinterlands, until finally the Arab slaver became a familiar ogre even among the peoples of central Africa. The first to organize the international slave trade, the Arabs were the last to give it up. And in Saudi Arabia to this day —although now discreetly and in masqueraded form—slaveholding and slave trading still exist.

Nevertheless it was not pagan Africans nor Moslem Arabs who made the slave trade the monumental enterprise it became, but Christian Europeans. Catholic, Anglican, Calvinist, Lutheran; Portuguese, Spanish, English, French,

Dutch, Danes, Swedes, Germans—much as they might quarrel among themselves, they could at least agree about the advantages to be gained from slaving; in that respect they quarreled only about who should gain the most. They maintained their piety throughout. For it was easy to demonstrate that to remove the African from his heathen environment and expose him to Christian influences would be greatly to the advantage of his immortal soul. Meantime there was money to be made.

SLIGHTLY to their credit, the Europeans did not begin their contacts with Africa with any such idea in mind. The Portuguese, who were the first to import slaves from the west African coast, began in an almost inadvertent way. Moslems held North Africa and all the Middle East, and hence could bar European merchants and missionaries from the rest of Africa and from Asia. Portugal began probing southward with two main objectives: to gain direct access to the products of the Sudan and the lands of the East; and to secure allies among the peoples there—by converting them to Christianity—for an attack on Islam from the flank and rear. Presumably one strong ally already existed: the legendary Prester John, Christian ruler of Ethiopia, who would eagerly join the Holy War if he could be found.

These expeditions began as early as 1415. By 1441 one had got as far as Cape Blanc (the tip of the northern coast of the present Islamic Republic of Mauritania), where its two young captains, Tristão and Gonçalves, captured 12 Africans before sailing back to Lisbon. The unfortunate dozen were trophies, but they also had commercial value—for slavery was not new to Portugal. The merchants of Lisbon, who had previously scoffed at Portugal's efforts to explore the African coast, now saw a chance to enrich themselves by importing Negroes and selling them as slaves in the less populated districts of the country. It was their money which financed Portugal's subsequent explorations.

These Portuguese voyages—whatever may be said of their mixed motives and eventual results —can only be described as epic and heroic. Within 15 years they had passed Cape Verde, the westernmost point of the Hump. By the 1470s they had explored the Hump's nether side and sailed south across the equator; by 1482, as we have seen, they were at the mouth of the Congo. Five years later Bartholomew Díaz sailed around the Cape of Good Hope. And before the century ended, Vasco da Gama sailed on up the east coast past the Horn and all the way to India.

On the east African coast the Portuguese adventurers encountered the Arabs and Swahilis, who by that time had established themselves in city-states along the coastal plain and adjoining islands for some 2,000 miles. By 1510, whether by conquest, threat or treaty, all of these towns had been brought under Portuguese hegemony. Finally, at the end of the 17th Century, incessant wars and assorted troubles caused the Portuguese to relinquish to the Arabs the coasts of what are now Tanganyika, Kenya and Somalia, but they clung to the rest, a stretch some 1,500 miles long. There they remain today, in the nearly 300,000-square-mile province called Mozambique.

MEANWHILE, on the west coast they had established forts and trading posts, or "factories," all the way from Cape Blanc down to Angola, and from there slaves had begun to flow in sizable numbers—probably at the rate of thousands a year by 1500—the west coast being preferred over the east because it was so much simpler to get the cargoes back alive and healthy to Portugal. By the mid-1500s, according to an official census, the traffic was so heavy that slaves comprised 10 per cent of Lisbon's population.

With the discovery of the New World, the pace quickened greatly. Columbus' voyage for Spain in 1492 was followed in 1500 by Cabral's claim of Brazil for Portugal. The sequence of the colonization and exploitation of the new lands, of the wars and politicking by which England, France and Holland established their dominions there, is too well known to need any exposition here. What should be kept in mind, however, is that the nature of the colonial economy, as it developed during the next centuries, created an insatiable need for manpower.

There were two main sources of wealth: mining and the cultivation of field crops. The Spanish, who were precluded from interfering with the Portuguese monopoly of Africa and its slave trade by a series of papal bulls and treaties in the latter part of the 15th Century, were in urgent need of manpower for their colonies. They tried American Indians as laborers, but for a variety of reasons the Indians were not satisfactory. So Spain entered the market for African slaves, commissioning the Portuguese to forward them from their African factories. By about 1550 the Spanish colonies were receiving some 4,000 slaves a year, most of them secured from the Portuguese factories of the west coast. Increasingly, they were sent into the fields—for the West Indies climate and soil proved to be ideal for the raising of sugar cane. Sugar had been a rare commodity in Europe. The market for it was huge, the profits were splendid and cane cultivation was dependent upon hand labor; soon the fields were aswarm with Africans.

For a while the slave trade remained a Portuguese-Spanish arrangement. The other nations had no stocks of domestic slaves to replenish, nor did they have colonies. In the latter part of the century, however, some of their private citizens began to take part in the slave trade: the great English merchant and adventurer Sir John Hawkins led the way with the first of a series of slaving voyages in 1562. And soon enough, when England, France and Holland began acquiring colonies in the 17th Century—colonies that produced sugar, tobacco and cotton—their

NOTED CAPTAIN, Vasco da Gama explored Africa's coast for Portugal. He was first to round the continent.

governments became involved. Through the agency of powerfully armed trading companies they began to fight the Portuguese, and later one another, for access to the best slaving areas and markets.

The Dutch, who were the first to challenge Portugal's monopoly, succeeded so spectacularly that for a while they were in control of the entire Guinea Coast, but later they had to share it with the Swedes, Germans, Danes and British. The British had factories and individual traders strung all the way from the mouth of the Gambia River around and below the Hump to the delta of the Niger River. The French took the areas around the Senegal River. The Portuguese finally found their west coast holdings above the equator reduced to the small enclave on the Hump now called Portuguese Guinea (just below Senegal), the Cape Verde Islands and the islands of Principe and São Tomé—anachronistic relics to which they have clung to this day. But, as on the east coast, the Portuguese stood fast in their southerly holdings and expanded inward from a thousand-mile coastline to bring under their control the tremendous area (10 times bigger than Pennsylvania) which became their present-day province of Angola.

The west African slave trade spanned a period of somewhat more than 400 years, beginning with Portugal's first effort in 1441, already described, and continuing until 1865. The number of Africans transported to the New World during that time is anybody's guess, for the records are scattered and incomplete, and in many cases have been lost. A conservative estimate, however, would be 15 million. Millions more died in passage, and their bodies were thrown overboard. Other millions died in the slave raids, on the march from the interior to the coast or at the factories where they were held before embarkation. It would be reasonable to suppose that the total number of victims, counting both the living and the dead, was on the order of 25 million—and some sources even put it at double that figure.

Who profited? The slaver, in fiction, was a retrograde specimen—a callous, sadistic, coarse-grained fellow whose personal character and professional activities were deplored by all men of taste and sensibility. The facts are quite different. The great slavers—those who employed the raiders, drivers and captains—were men of substance and often of exceedingly high station. The kings of Spain and Portugal held royal monopolies on the trade to their dominions; these were parceled out on contract to large firms in return for a share of the profits and a fixed fee per *pièce d'Inde*, a unit of measurement representing one prime adult slave landed in good condition or a group of inferior ones.

THUS, for example, in 1702 the Spanish *asiento*, or contract, was let to the French Guinea Company on terms that called for delivery of 38,000 slaves over a 10-to-12-year period, the king to receive 33⅓ crowns for each *pièce*. When England defeated the French in the War of the Spanish Succession early in the 18th Century, the spoils included not only the Hudson Bay area and other territorial gains, but the right to the Spanish *asiento*. The profits were shared: half to English traders, a fourth to the king of Spain and the other fourth to the English royal treasury.

The *asiento* was a necessary device for Spain because that country had only insignificant possessions below the Sahara. The Portuguese government, on the other hand, could reasonably attempt to keep the whole trade and all the profits of the Brazilian market in the hands of its own officials and companies. This aim mainly succeeded, but sometimes it had to be compromised because Portuguese slavers, try as they would, could not supply enough *pièces* to meet the demand. With the discovery of gold and diamonds, and above all with the growth of its sugar industry, Brazil was consuming more than 10,000 slaves a year by 1700, and fairly often slave ships that were headed for Brazil had to load at French, British and Dutch factories or, more expensively, at the big wholesale markets that had grown up in Cuba and some of the other West Indies.

OBVIOUSLY it was not just the Spanish and the Portuguese ruling classes who enriched themselves by the slave trade. Lords and gentlemen, bankers, merchants, shipowners and landowners in other countries and in the Americas became wealthy in the trade, or by catering to it, or through the ownership and use of its human chattels. There were Yankee slavers, the most numerous being from Newport; slave ships off-loaded at all the southern ports. The profits, spreading out through the economic systems in a thousand ways, creating industries and capital funds, contributed substantially to the economic development that took place in Europe and the New World during the 17th and 18th Centuries.

But it was not just the Europeans and Americans who profited from the slave trade. There were the Arabs and Arab-Berbers and Arab-Berberized-Negroes of the western Sudan who, with their previous monopoly broken, soon found their eyes turning toward the coast. And there were the Arab and Swahili potentates and slave dealers of the east coast, whose palmiest days came in the 19th Century when they had the market (by then mostly illicit) to themselves. And not the least—nor least significantly—there were the black Africans themselves. Not the slaves, of course, but the Africans who procured and sold them to the various slave-trading nations.

As noted in the previous chapter, the decline of the Sudanic kingdoms had been matched by the rise of kingdoms along the Guinea Coast. Like the Sudanic kingdoms, these arose because of trade opportunities, which increasingly and then overwhelmingly revolved around slaving. To summarize, in practically all the

THE U.S. SLAVE TRADE

TOTAL IMPORTED

The exact number of African slaves brought to the United States from 1619, when the first cargo of 20 Africans landed at Jamestown, Virginia, to 1858, when the last slave ship unloaded 450 near Brunswick, Georgia, is not known. At the outbreak of the Revolution, there were an estimated 500,000 slaves in the 13 colonies; in 1860, there were 3,980,000 slaves and 500,-000 free Negroes in the country.

THE SHIPPERS

Slave ships operated out of almost all the coastal states in the early days of slaving, but particularly from New England. Rhode Island alone had 150 vessels in the trade in 1770. After 1808, when Congress forbade further importation, smuggling flourished. The slavers maintained offshore island depots where slaves were kept pending sale. Just prior to the Civil War, an estimated 15,000 slaves a year were still being smuggled into the country.

THE DOMESTIC MARKET

The internal slave trade was limited in pre-Revolutionary days but became a large-scale business after 1800, as the plantation system spread to the opening Southwest. Trading companies established assembly depots in Virginia and other northerly states of the South, stocking them with surplus slaves bought in the area. The slaves were then either shipped to the Southwest aboard vessels which traveled around Florida into the Gulf of Mexico, or herded overland and sent down the Mississippi.

THE TRADING CENTERS

Auctions were held everywhere in the South, but primarily in the cities of Alexandria, Charleston, Mobile, Natchez, New Orleans, Richmond and Savannah. A male slave could bring as much as $1,800 just before the Civil War.

THE INTERNAL VOLUME

Few statistics were kept. Exporting states were Kentucky, Maryland, Missouri, North Carolina, South Carolina and Virginia; importers included Arkansas, Florida and Texas. Alabama, Georgia, Louisiana, Mississippi and Tennessee both exported and imported. It is estimated that some 80,000 slaves, their total value coming to $59 million, changed hands each year during the 1850s.

cases the sequence went as follows: Europeans, arriving on the coast, made either a compact or a truce with the most powerful tribal chief or kinglet of the neighborhood, built their fortresses or factories with his aid or consent and began trading their goods for the local produce. For ordinary items in easy supply they traded with the general populace, but otherwise they dealt with the chief or his subchiefs and deputies, since it was the chiefs who monopolized the valuables—the gold and ivory and feathers and, of course, the slaves.

HOW did the chiefs get the slaves? To some extent they got them from among their own people. The more powerful chiefs, as we saw earlier, tended to be autocrats: they could and did make slavery the punishment for infractions of tribal rules. To a larger extent the chiefs obtained slaves by raiding weaker neighboring tribes. And to a very considerable extent they acquired them by trading with the chiefs and kinglets and kings of the regions back of the coast, who had slaves and knew where to get more of them and who also, of course, had an appetite for the European trade goods.

It was precisely the latter point that led to the creation of the new coastal kingdoms during the 17th and 18th Centuries. The interior tribes, through their long exposure to the Arab-Berber influences from the Sudan, had developed greater political and technological sophistication than the Guinea Coast tribes and, once having realized that these backward people held the key to the "riches" of Europe, they invaded and conquered them. Occasionally it worked the other way and the coastal people, with their newly acquired stock of firearms and European sophistication, managed to dominate the people of the interior. But mostly the movement was from the interior toward the coast.

From their chieftaincy which was at Abomey, for example, about 60 miles from the coast, a segment of the Fon tribe conquered the region to the south, thereby forming the important kingdom of Dahomey. Similarly the Akan state of Kumasi managed by war and political maneuver to dominate all its neighbors and create the powerful confederate kingdom of Ashanti on the Gold Coast.

These and their several counterparts were slaving states. The trade was not forced on them: on the contrary, they fought for the privilege. Their importance within the system is indicated by one eloquent and extraordinary fact. Until the early 19th Century, Europeans still knew very little of Tropical Africa except its coastal fringes. In most of the region no white man had ever set foot.

This does not excuse the role of the Europeans in the slave trade, of course, but it does illuminate a truth that some African nationalists are inclined to overlook. Slavery was not specifically a crime of Europeans against Africans. It was a crime of Europeans and Arabs *and* Africans and, in the truest sense, it was a crime of mankind.

The people of the Guinea Coast and contiguous regions have had an important part in the modern African nationalist movement, as we will subsequently see. What is more interesting in the present context, however, is the role played by the coastal people in the slave trade with the North American continent—hence in the origins of the 10 per cent of United States citizens who are of African descent.

This is a subject that necessarily involves some guesswork, of course. Slavery was almost universal in Africa. Sooner or later, slaves from almost every part of Africa arrived at the coastal factories, from which they might then be dispatched to almost any part of the New World. In view of the racial mixing described in earlier chapters, we can safely assume that the Afro-American population contains traces of all the major elements that made up the population of the African continent, from the Negro

to the Pygmy, the Bushman and the Arab.

It seems evident from the number of long-legged Afro-American athletes (such as "Wilt the Stilt" Chamberlain, the nonpareil basketball player) that there is more than a trace of the elongated Nilote. There is bound to be a significant element of Bantu, since these peoples are so widespread in the southern half of the continent and make up almost the whole population of Angola and the Congo. From Angola and adjacent Congo regions, Portugal finally managed to ship an estimated five million slaves to the New World—one third of the whole number who landed there alive.

Most of the slaves shipped by the Portuguese were sent to Brazil or to the Spanish colonies, but a certain number were consigned to the markets in the West Indies. No doubt some of these, or their descendants, finally were taken to the United States, where the importing of slaves was not forbidden until 1808.

Nevertheless, as recent research has shown, the preponderant sources of such imports lay along the south side of the Hump. Quite simply, powerful tribes there made war on one another or on weaker tribes of their area, and the captives were sent to market. The attrition was huge, but it was spread over centuries. Also, this is one of the more fertile areas of Africa and can support a large population—as it does today (about one third of the continent's total). So the supply of potential captives remained large and reasonably steady. The Guinea Coast and an adjoining belt extending perhaps 300 miles into the interior is by all odds the most important ethnic source of present-day Afro-Americans. It is especially interesting to note that the west African Negroes who live in this area are among the most intelligent, energetic and creative people in all Tropical Africa.

TO BE SOLD, on board the Ship *Bance-Island*, on tuesday the 6th of *May* next, at *Aſhley-Ferry*; a choice cargo of about 250 fine healthy NEGROES, juſt arrived from the Windward & Rice Coaſt. —The utmoſt care has already been taken, and ſhall be continued, to keep them free from the leaſt danger of being infected with the SMALL-POX, no boat having been on board, and all other communication with people from *Charles-Town* prevented. *Auſtin, Laurens, & Appleby.*

N. B. Full one Half of the above Negroes have had the SMALL-POX in their own Country.

NOTICE OF SALE posted in Charleston, South Carolina, assures buyers that new slaves are free of disease.

SLAVE PRISON survives grim and abandoned (*left*) in Senegal. After buying up slaves, merchants would use it to store their property securely until a slave ship arrived.

SLAVE CONVOY of men (*opposite*) is driven from the interior to Cape Coast Castle, a British trading post. Traders would load them on ships and sail for the West Indies.

A Sterile Partnership in a Cruel Trade

Like any business, the traffic in slaves was extremely methodical. In west Africa, powerful chiefs were the suppliers, certain coastal tribes were the middlemen and European companies operated the trading stations. Shipping slaves was largely a problem in storage and maintenance. But the African-European trade partnership did not open Africa to Europe. Only after the partnership was broken did Europeans undertake widespread exploration of the interior.

HUMAN CARGO on a slave ship is taken on deck and exercised under the lash to maintain the captives' bodily fitness. Below decks, other slaves wait their turn in the three-foot-high space, where they were kept shackled for as much as 16 hours at a stretch. Netting was set up—not always successfully—to bar suicidal leaps overboard.

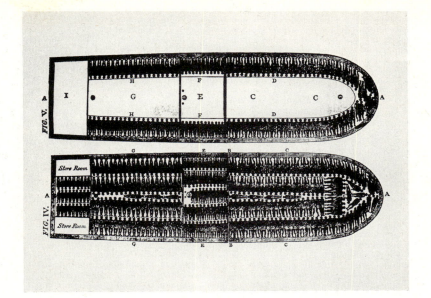

BRUTAL ECONOMY, a frugal method for stowing slaves is outlined in this 19th Century diagram (*right*). Circulated in Britain, France and the U.S., the diagram was widely used by abolitionists in their antislavery campaign.

ANTISLAVERY ATTACK by the British schooner *Pickle* against the sinking slave ship *Bolodora* is shown in this 19th Century print. After 1807 the British fleet began patrolling the seas to blockade the traffic in slaves.

METHODICAL TEAM, Captain John Hanning Speke (*left*) and Captain James Grant determined in 1862 that Lake Victoria was the true source of the White Nile—thereby solving one of the world's oldest mysteries. However, rival explorers with more colorful temperaments had other theories, and the discovery went unaccepted for years.

ROMANTIC ADVENTURER, Sir Richard Burton, scholar, author and swordsman, discovered Lake Tanganyika in 1858 during a lifetime spent in a half-mad quest for the exotic. Brilliant, eloquent and prodigiously erudite, he wrote superb travel books that whetted Victorian England's appetite for more news from the dark continent.

DARING EXPLORERS brought

the unknown interior to the attention

of Europe in the 19th Century

IRON-WILLED JOURNALIST, Henry Morton Stanley began his career as an African explorer in 1869 when the New York *Herald* assigned him to search for Dr. Livingstone. Hard-bitten, ruthless and avid for fame, he made an epic first voyage down the Congo in 1876-1877 and carved out a private empire for the King of Belgium.

GODLY IDEALIST, Dr. David Livingstone was a missionary who became one of the greatest of the African explorers. For nearly 30 years of privation and loneliness he trekked and mapped the vast, tedious reaches of central Africa in hopes that his fellow missionaries would follow in his steps to bring Africans the word of God.

At a funeral in a central African village, ecstatic mourners lift a live child in the air as the feasting and dancing reaches a frenzied

climax. Such rites insure that the deceased will depart contented.

6

All-Pervading World of the Spirit

TO the same degree that the slavers in Africa represented western civilization at its worst, the missionaries have represented it at its best and most constructive. From all parts of western Europe and America they have gone to Africa, not only to spread the gospel of salvation but to show the way to a better life, and often have lost their own lives to disease and hardship in the attempt. Many thousands of them have entered Africa in the course of the centuries; hundreds of millions of Christian laymen, of practically all denominations and all western nations, have contributed through their church mission funds toward the support of their labors. With what results?

In a number of ways—magnificent. Medical missionaries like Dr. Albert Schweitzer have relieved untold suffering. With the help of government medical workers, they have begun to bring under control the worst of the diseases that traditionally have ravaged the populations. Teaching missionaries can see their handiwork in the emergence of desperately needed African professional and technical workers. Perhaps with qualified satisfaction they can see it also in the new Africa's political leaders, a large majority of whom received their early education at mission schools. Christian and western ideas consequently are widely diffused among the people who, in a majority of the countries, will be most influential in determining the future.

In certain other ways the results have been deplorable. With an excess of zeal and an incomprehension—part pure ignorance, part deriving from sectarian credos and bigotry—of the traditional values of African life, some missionaries have been intent on uprooting old customs and pasting over them a veneer of religious observance, substituting form for content. The effect has been to dry up the spontaneity of African life or to turn it in perverse directions—some of them charged with anti-church, anti-white and anti-West feelings.

BUT what may seem more surprising, in view of the large and mostly sympathetic effort that has gone into their work, is that Christian missionaries have had little success in converting the African masses even to nominal Christianity, let alone the real thing. Some 20 per cent of the people of Tropical Africa are professing Christians. About the same number are Moslems, while 60 per cent are "heathens." There are few reasons for thinking that this situation will change in favor of Christianity in the foreseeable future. On the contrary, nearly five centuries after the arrival of the first missionaries, the Christian church as a whole is on the defensive in Tropical Africa.

To some extent, of course, this is a reflection of the new tide of nationalism. Christianity came to Africa from the same sources as colonialism. The church often was the close colleague of the government in administering the affairs of the people. Inevitably it had suffered from its identification as "the white man's religion"—a religion whose principles the white man often violated in his daily life and in his behavior toward the Africans. In

1910 Charles Domingo, an African preacher who was the leader of an independent church in Nyasaland, published a manifesto whose import would still ring true to many Africans:

"The three combined bodies, Missionaries, Government, and Companies, or gainers of money, do form the same rule to look upon the native with mockery eyes. It sometimes startles us to see that the three combined bodies are from Europe, and along with them there is a title, 'CHRISTENDOM' . . . . If we had power enough to communicate ourselves to Europe we would advise them not to call themselves 'Christendom' but 'Europeandom'. . . . the life of the three combined bodies is altogether too cheaty, too thefty, too mockery. . . ."

But there is another, considerably more important matter involved. Christian doctrine is in many ways truly a foreign import. It cuts across African social patterns and is antithetical to most of Africa's traditional religious beliefs —to the African's view of himself, his fellows, his natural environment and the whole universe in which he lives, dies and lives again.

This traditional (and still predominant) view is infinitely various in detail, differing from tribe to tribe. Nevertheless, there is an over-all pattern, or perhaps more accurately a series of interlocking patterns, which can be described.

THROUGHOUT history, as we have seen, the African has been the victim of unpredictable and frequently malign forces. Drought and flood, pastures that failed and soils that wore out, diseases, dangerous wild animals, marauding invaders who stole his lands and goods and women, raiders who arrived mysteriously and took him away to unknown places—all these things exposed the African to imminent disaster yet had no discernible causes. Neither, of course, did thunder and lightning, the winds that blew, the sun that shone and all those other natural phenomena among which he lived so intimately and had his being. In the midst of irrationality and mystery it was easy for him to deduce (as "primitive" peoples in other parts of the world invariably have done) that these events were manipulated by invisible beings, powers, forces; further, that these forces took an interest in his affairs, rewarding him when they were pleased and punishing him if displeased; and hence that there must be ways by which he could enlist their favor for himself and their disfavor against his enemies.

THUS the African constructed a spiritual universe, an unseen counterpart of the visible universe and an extension of it beyond his range of sight and experience. Things were not merely what they seemed; rocks, rivers, mountains, clouds, ants and elephants—all of these had not only an outer and tangible form but an inner force or soul-stuff, a spirit, that made them what they were; moreover, many believed that these spirits were conscious and had feelings and emotions, including vanity, anger and vengefulness. (This belief that natural objects are inhabited by souls is known as animism.) Their powers were arranged in a logical hierarchy in which those of man himself occupied a rather dubious intermediate position. A human could kick a pebble or cut brush for firewood with impunity, but if he dislodged a boulder or cut down a tree he would need to placate its spirits with flattering apologies and ceremonials, for these were strong enough to do him harm.

The larger objects and phenomena in nature commanded his respect and fear and, to the extent that he made use of them, his reverent hope. He made ceremonial obeisance to the sun, moon and stars, the sea, rivers, mountains, caves, forests, deserts, thunder, lightning and rain—not really worshiping nature but trying to invite the good will of the manifold powers within it, or at least their neutrality.

Where was God and what was He? Many tribes had a conception of a Supreme Being or a Prime Creator. His character was benevolent, and He had been the original source of all things. However, having created the universe, He reigned over it dispassionately and seldom intervened in events. He neither gave favors to men nor required anything of them and was appealed to only in time of great need.

BELOW him, however, there was a large pantheon of lesser gods, spirits and powers. Their names and natures varied from tribe to tribe, but in general each had charge of a particular aspect of earthly existence. Like the spirits of the rocks and rills, these great, earth-spanning spirits formed a hierarchy, those of the greatest prestige being the ones, naturally, which controlled the things important to the particular tribe: fishing, stock-herding, crop-raising or warfare, as the case might be.

Forces that influenced fertility occupied an extremely important position for obvious reasons: infant mortality was high, big families were desirable for their labor and as a form of old-age security, and disease and war took a large toll. Since human procreation was associated with the fertility of crops and herds, the procreative act and the apparatus and events

---

A KIKUYU PRAYER FOR RAIN

Reverend Elder [God] who lives on Kere-Nyaga,
You who make mountains tremble
   and rivers flood;
We offer to you this sacrifice that you may
   bring us rain.
People and children are crying; sheep, goats,
   and cattle are crying.
Mwene-Nyaga, we beseech you,
   with the blood and fat of this lamb

which we are going to sacrifice to you.
Refined honey and milk we have brought for you.
We praise you in the same way as our forefathers
   used to praise you under this very same tree,
   and you heard them and brought them rain.
We beseech you to accept this, our sacrifice,
   and bring us rain of prosperity.
Response: Peace, we beseech you, Ngai,
   peace be with us.

related to it were endowed with extraordinary significance and became the subject of intricate rules, ceremonials and symbolism. Europeans, encountering these rites, often decided that the African was hypersexual, and missionaries generally were scandalized.

And in fact, of course, some of these practices, especially those connected with puberty, were senselessly cruel, degrading and dangerous. But what was often overlooked was that these had evolved naturally from the circumstances in which the African lived, and that they made excellent sense to him.

WITHIN this spirit world there also lived the ancestors. The African, with his belief in a universal inner reality, took human immortality for granted. The human soul, after physical death, simply acquired a different condition. Probably it went to heaven for a while —but this was an ill-defined place, most likely in the sky but perhaps on a mountaintop or simply somewhere, "over there." In any case, in the spirit world, the soul joined some of the other ancestors, met some of the gods and associated with other spirits, souls and forces.

Sooner or later it came home to its own village, often to its own hut, and stayed there with the family. When its turn came (and this was another reason for desiring many children), it would be reborn in the family as a new baby. Thus an African could be his own grandfather. Meantime the soul took a close interest in family affairs. It wished to be consulted about them. It also expected decent respect and nourishment: food set out for it at mealtime, libations poured and words spoken in its honor. If satisfied, the soul would protect the family and bring it good fortune. If offended, it took vengeance by bringing accidents, sickness and general bad fortune to the guilty neglectful living.

Ancestors, like all other spirits, had their own hierarchy, and this reflected their earthly status. When a chief died, his soul consorted with those of other chiefs and kings, and they all consorted, in their degrees of importance, with the more powerful spirits or gods, with whom they could intercede for the welfare of the village or tribe. A living chief was himself semi-divine or divine. Messages from him would be received with respect and attention by dead chiefs and other influential spirits, and they would reply with help or advice. Thus the roles of chief and high priest tended to be combined, and in many tribes this led to the glorification of the chief as a living god who embodied the whole vital force of the tribe.

Hence he had to be obeyed; he required flattery, obeisance, gifts and various symbolic attestations of his awesome status. His bare feet might not be allowed to touch the ground, for instance; or no one must see him eat, or he must be fed by others; or he must speak only through "interpreters" instead of directly.

HIS death quite often involved human sacrifices. The King of Bunyoro, for instance, as C. G. Seligman relates in *Races of Africa,* was "buried in a grave lined with the living bodies of his wives and retainers, whose arms and legs had previously been broken to prevent their escape." Similarly, in neighboring Buganda, the king's death "was announced by the extinction of the sacred fire which burned near the entrance of the royal enclosure and the strangling of the chief who had charge of it. The king's body . . . was buried with many victims; five months later the jawbone was taken from the skull and placed beside the umbilical cord (carefully preserved during lifetime) in a temple specially built for it, where it was thenceforth guarded by the ex-queen."

The right to such courtesies was accompanied by hazards, however, for, since the king was the incarnation of the tribe's collective spirit, any misfortune that came to the tribe must be due to a defect in *him.* Among many tribes rain making was one of the chief's most important functions. When this or other important powers weakened or failed, the king could be deposed or even killed. Again from Seligman: ". . . it was in order that the spirit might be housed in a thoroughly healthy body that the habitual practice of the Shilluk [a tribal nation in Sudan] was to slay their king directly he showed signs of ill-health, or even of such gradual senescence as was evidenced by inability to satisfy his large number of wives. For it was felt that . . . with the diminishing vitality of the king the cattle would sicken and fail to bear their increase, the crops would rot in the fields, and men, stricken with disease, would die in ever-increasing numbers. . . . The leading part in killing the king was taken by members of certain families, called *oro-ro*. . . . Perhaps in quite recent times the king was strangled, certainly a few generations ago he was walled up in a hut and allowed to perish."

With such a busy and complex spirit world and such a load of problems (Should the son of O marry the daughter of Z? Was the lion that ate T's baby just a lion or the spirit of a dead chief? Was it going to rain tomorrow?), even the god-king needed consultants and special assistants. These might include priests in the service of a deity, the trance-mediums through whom the spirits spoke, and soothsayers or diviners who, by means of such devices as casting an assortment of small bones on the ground and studying the relationships into which they fell, could foretell the future. There might be a number of such functionaries spread through the kingdom or tribe serving regional and village needs. And, of course, there were witch doctors.

This is a term so widely misunderstood that it needs precise definition, beginning with the role of magic in traditional African society. The spirit world, in this view, is responsive not only to cajoleries and supplications; it also can be manipulated and in a sense commanded by means of certain occult formulas—the mixing of certain materials together or the saying of special words accompanied by special gestures. In the same degree, impersonal spiritual forces—not gods, not souls, not entities of any sort, but indefinable supernatural emanations that have the power to help or harm—can be controlled and directed by similar means. All this, the techniques and the results, is what is meant by "magic." To some extent, every African used these formulas and was a magician. However, it was a recondite subject in which knowledge in truth was power; and so branches of the science grew, and people became specialists.

Human nature being as perverse in Africa as anyplace else, some people became sorcerers. They were specialists in magical practices aimed at doing harm to others, such as causing a man's crops to fail, his wives to be barren, or a multitude of misfortunes ranging from a stubbed toe to death itself. Indeed, it was widely believed that death, far from being inevitable, was not even normal—a man died because his defenses had been overwhelmed by sorcery.

The sorcerers had many weapons. For example, "the power of the bone": a magical bone used in some parts of Africa could cause a man to sicken and die simply by being pointed at him. Or magic powder, perhaps sprinkled on the victim as he slept, or around his hut: "At the very sight of such powder men have been known to die," Geoffrey Parrinder, the author of *African*

MAGICAL OBJECTS OF AFRICA

Charm, or "medicine": an inanimate object or collection of objects believed to possess occult power. A charm can be a natural object or a man-made ornament, but in either case its power is inherent and impersonal, affecting all who come into contact with it.

Talisman: an object, frequently small enough to be worn on the body, believed to bring good fortune.

Amulet: like a talisman, but used to avert evil rather than to bring luck. Talismans and amulets often rank as charms, but they do not necessarily possess occult power; a charm, however, may be employed as either talisman or amulet, often combining both positive and negative qualities.

Fetish: an object "possessed" by a spiritual being. Like a charm, a fetish may be used to bring good fortune or to avert evil, but unlike a charm, it does not work automatically; its activity depends on the will of the spirit embodied in it.

Juju: literally a "little doll" or image. But the word is often used to describe magical powers or magic itself.

The All-Pervading World of the Spirit

Traditional Religion, has said. Or, perhaps most terrifying of all, charms containing something that had been intimately associated with the proposed victim or, even better, physically connected to him, such as his nail parings or a lock of his hair. Hence such things had to be carefully disposed of in private lest they fall into the wrong hands—many chiefs even employed attendants to collect their spittle when they appeared in public and, from the chewing of kola nuts or other causes, felt the urge to expectorate. Mothers took care to bury the placenta and umbilical cord after they had given birth, for, of course, nothing could be more potently dangerous to the welfare of the child if secured by an enemy—such an enemy, for example, as a barren or unattractive and jealous co-wife. The latter might know how to fashion the fatal charm herself, but otherwise she would go to the sorcerer and would pay him a fee for his instructions or handiwork.

THE African sorcerer was greatly feared, but his powers were greatly respected. The African witch, on the other hand, was equally feared but loathed. She (witches almost always were women) had within herself a power of evil which worked spontaneously, and it often worked even without her own awareness. Simply by existing, the witch could cause all manner of troubles within the village and the tribe. What made the witch most hateful, however, was that she preyed on souls.

This occurred at night, when people's souls (so the belief went) left their sleeping bodies, journeyed about and had a series of adventures —an experience that we call dreams. The soul of the witch, in its own nightly wanderings, was possessed with the dreadful appetite and the power to eat these other souls, perhaps returning to feast night after night until there was nothing left and the progressively weakened bodies died. Witches were especially fond of young and tender souls—even those in their own families—and a group of them might easily devour the soul of a baby in a single night, and then leave the body dead or dying—as was

witnessed by the extremely high infant mortality rates in Africa.

Thus, by day and by night, the African was threatened by evil forces, against which he would have felt powerless except for the equally strong countervailing forces that were commanded by the witch doctor. Against the "black magic" of the sorcerer and witch, he employed "white magic" (the terms are indigenous to Africa and have nothing to do with skin color). Through his own specialized techniques, which were fully as arcane as those of the sorcerer, he could undo the latter's spells and expose witches —generally to their surprise and mortification, for they were seldom aware of their nighttime cravings or of their deadly emanations of witchcraft substance.

FREQUENTLY a trance-medium, almost always a soothsayer, the witch doctor was an all-round master of the occult. He was an expert on fabricating healthy, lucky and protective talismans, amulets and other charms; on the varieties and uses of "medicine horns" (animal horns stuffed with magic substances), dances, chants, masks and incantations; and on the uses of an elaborate pharmacopoeia of herbs, berries and other natural medicines such as pulverized monkey skull, lion dung and cow's fetus.

Leaving aside such doubtful matters as ancestral intercession, the fact remains that both black and white magic often did (and still do) produce dramatic effects on human health and behavior. To the modern medical scientist, the explanation is not too difficult. Often the witch doctor's kit actually contains some items of medical value, just as the sorcerer's contains some real poisons. But far more important is the scientifically proven potency of belief. The "power of the bone" is an example of the power of suggestion—the same mechanism that accounts, in devious and indirect ways, for numerous and often quite serious psychosomatic illnesses and for the spectacular "cures" associated with hypnosis and faith healings.

The African, with a perhaps instinctive understanding of the Power of Negative Thinking, generally arranged somehow—perhaps even inadvertently, by a nuance of phrase or a trace of a triumphant or guilty look—that his selected victim would know or would suspect that he had been cursed; in the common phrase, had "had juju put on him." But otherwise the enterprise carried itself: it was the belief in magic that made the magic work, and the fact that it worked reinforced the belief. And although magic might be terrifying, it was also in a way satisfying, for it explained so many of the otherwise inexplicable fortunes and misfortunes of life.

Indeed, the whole structure of African traditional beliefs—ancestors, divine chieftaincy, great spirits, gods, forces, emanations, reincarnation—possesses a great deal of internal logic. As Freud pointed out in his study of primitive religions, *Totem and Taboo*, they comprise a wonderfully satisfying faith because they supply an explanation for *everything*.

THE forces of tradition run deep and strong in Africa—a point worth reiterating again and yet again—and Christian doctrine contradicts the traditional beliefs directly and beyond compromise. The ideas of a personal universal God, of the primary importance of the individual, of the forgiveness of one's enemies, of the brotherhood of man and of monogamous marriage—such things are exotic indeed to the African. When he accepts them, he very often does so with private reservations, taking what suits him but still keeping what is useful from his earlier set of beliefs. The result is a proliferation of syncretic sects, which are Christian in name but sometimes are totally unrecognizable in actual creed and behavior.

Islam, the other great religious import, confronts far fewer obstacles. Monotheism is one obstacle; yet Allah is not too hard to identify with the Prime Creator who presides impersonally over the spirit world of so many tribes. Islamic doctrines are relatively compact, simple and uniform—as compared with the competitive welter of ideas and rituals offered by the Christian denominations. Islam is less strict and makes fewer demands; it does not interfere with cherished customs; and, despite its monotheism, it allows room for the spirit world of African tradition.

As Seligman has pointed out regarding the Tuareg tribesmen of the Sahara: ". . . animism is part of everyday belief; it is commonly accepted that below the surface the desert is peopled by . . . supernatural beings who delight in playing mischievous pranks on the wayfarer, and all unexplained phenomena are referred to invisible agencies, while the mysterious droning . . . heard on a still night in many parts of the desert is the voice of the jinn [supernatural beings] conversing among themselves."

ALSO, there is the Islamic phenomenon of *baraka*. The word literally means "blessing" and is applied to a mysterious force that resides in holy men and leaders, particularly those who claim descent from Mohammed. A chief who has plenty of *baraka* can bring his people great good fortune, or by misusing it he can do great harm. Continued misfortunes indicate that his *baraka* may be failing and that he would do well to think of retiring. The same idea, as we saw, is common in African tradition. Islamic notions of divine kingship, of political absolutism, of the organization of society in hierarchies, of the importance of the community and family, of the glory of battle, of the sweetness of revenge and of much else find counterparts in African beliefs. And, of course, Islam permits polygamy and concubinage. Finally, although it was Arab in the first place, Islam has long since—as we saw in earlier chapters—become thoroughly Africanized. There is no remaining tinge of "white man's religion" about it, and traditionally there is no color bar in Islam. In Africa it belongs to the black man, and its missionaries are almost always men of African blood.

Accordingly, Christianity's greatest challenge is Islam. At recent comparative rates of growth, Islam probably will be well ahead in the contest within a few years, and it seems entirely possible that the next 50 years or so will find an Africa that is predominantly Islamic.

The Deeply Divided Realm of Worship

Among people suddenly torn from their ancient moorings, religion has become an explosive force. Magical practices which formed part of traditional faith have been retained by city dwellers as a way of proclaiming their loyalty to things African. Christianity itself, for all its superb work in teaching and healing (*left and opposite*), has supplied a sword to numerous African "messiahs" who use the Bible's language to preach against the European "pharaohs." Islam, racially tolerant and long-entrenched, now energetically seeks —and wins—converts. But though Islam may triumph in the future, millions of Africans today have no consistent faith at all.

ISLAM'S HOLD on millions
has been strengthened and extended
in recent years as the idea gains currency
among many that this adaptable faith
is the only alternative to both paganism
and "white man's Christianity"

BOWING inside a modernistic mosque (*above*) newly erected to emphasize Islam's sympathy with progressive ideas, students at a Nigerian teachers college gather for Friday observances.

KNEELING in a row toward Mecca after parking their bicycles, a group of Nigerian Moslems (*left*) perform their daily prayers, one of the few demands made by Islam on its followers.

DRILLING children in the Koran, a teacher at a traditional school in Timbuktu (*opposite*) makes his young pupils commit to memory portions of the holy book set down on wooden tablets.

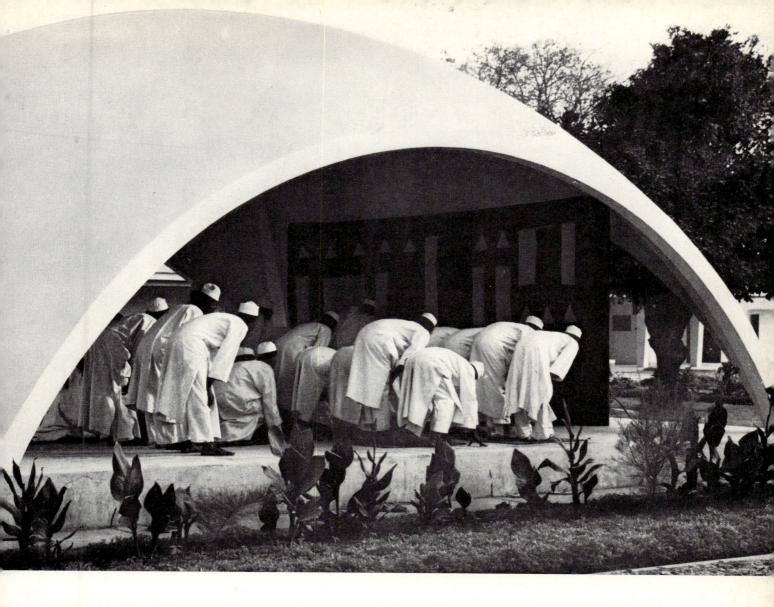

WIZENED ELDER dances with three young girls who are celebrating the completion of the tortuous ceremonies that initiate them into the tribe as full-fledged women.

ENTRANCED PRIESTESS of a village sways to the beat of drums (*opposite*) during a ritual slaughter of a sheep. The sacrifices are intended to placate the god of the cult.

THE DANCE, *performed with striking skill to the syncopated beat of drums, is a ritual drama that links men with the lurking world of the spirit*

CROUCHING LOW, two Liberian girls perform the quick, furious steps of a dance of celebration. Even when Africa's dances are frenzied and extravagant, they are likely to be as intricate and disciplined as any western ballet. Traditionally, much of the dancing had a religious function—to insure fertility, to induce a fruitful harvest or to placate the village gods. Today the dance sturdily survives as a quasi-religious means of ecstatic release.

107

WOODEN FLUTE is one of many wind instruments traditionally used by African musicians, who have evolved a kind of music in which complicated rhythms are prominent. Most U.S. jazz has its roots in the music of Africa.

7

A Unique Artistic Heritage

A FEW years ago Sir Philip Mitchell, former Governor of Kenya, in an essay on "Africa and the West in Historical Perspective," described what seemed to him to be some of the main characteristics of Africa at the beginning of the Colonial era. He wrote: "The West found itself in control of millions of people who had never invented or adopted an alphabet or even any form of hieroglyphic writing. They had no numerals, no almanac or calendar, no notation of time or measurements of length, capacity, or weight, no currency, no external trade except slaves and ivory . . . no plough, no wheel and no means of transportation except human head

porterage on land and dugout canoes on rivers and lakes. These people had built nothing, nothing of any kind, in any material more durable than mud, poles, and thatch. With a few notable exceptions, there were no units of government throughout the area larger than the tribe, and the tribe might amount only to a few thousand people and have half a dozen contending chiefs . . . Great numbers wore no clothes at all; others wore bark cloth or hides and skins."

Some time after Sir Philip, a poet from Martinique named Aimé Césaire composed these lines, which might almost have been designed as poetic counterpoint to Mitchell's theme:

> *Hurray for those who never invented
>   anything*
> *Hurray for those who never explored
>   anything*
> *Hurray for those who never conquered
>   anything*
> *But who, in awe, give themselves up to the
>   essence of things*
> *Ignorant of the shell, but seized by the
>   rhythm of things*
> *Not intent on conquest, but playing the
>   play of the world.*
>
> *My négritude is neither a tower
>   nor a cathedral*
> *It plunges into the red flesh of the earth*
> *It plunges into the burning flesh
>   of the sky*
> *It pierces the opaque prostration by its
>   upright patience.*

THESE two statements, based on the same premise, opposite in their attitudes toward it, are almost classic expressions of two prevalent points of view about Africa's cultural heritage. The first is that the heritage is so meager that the role the Europeans have played in Africa—granted that, as Sir Philip Mitchell said, "It might have been better, that it has its blemishes and faults"—has on the whole been one of civilizers and teachers; that this has been not only a worthy but a necessary function, a kind of cultural rescue; and, by extension, that more of the same will be necessary until such time as African society has absorbed western cultural patterns and remade itself in their image.

Obviously this point of view offers easy opportunities for rationalizing the slowest possible withdrawal of European political control, and the traveler will hear it in endless versions and variations wherever Europeans have settled in Africa in significant numbers. But this does not alter the fact that often, perhaps even usually, it is an honest opinion that is held by honest and well-meaning men, Sir Philip Mitchell among them. The group includes not only

Europeans but some African political leaders.

The other viewpoint is that Africa, not simply in spite of but almost because of its failure to attain by itself the civilized attributes—because it had "never invented anything, explored anything, conquered anything"—possessed attributes of its own that were unique and precious and must be preserved and cultivated. The question was, "What?" This has been a very serious question indeed, a central question in the minds of some of Africa's most gifted leaders, and it has had serious and sometimes even bizarre consequences.

Among the latter one could mention the justification some years ago by the Kenya radical Jomo Kenyatta—a trained anthropologist, and resident of Britain and Europe for over 15 years—of clitoridectomy in the initiation rites of the girls of his native Kikuyu tribe, a custom whose virtue seemingly lay in the fact that it *was* a custom of his people. Without his fanaticism (Kenyatta was convicted as the alleged inspirer of the murderous Mau Mau movement), others, most notably Kwame Nkrumah of Ghana, have tried to build the political and social structure of the new Africa on their concept of "the African Personality," believing that there is, or ought to be, a way of doing things that is distinctively and valuably African.

THE idea of *négritude* represents the same desire, the same experimental and groping belief, cast in terms that are somewhat more esthetic and spiritual. Invented by Césaire, not an African by birth but a French-speaking man of African descent, the term was picked up from the poem quoted above and seized with enthusiasm by some of the leaders of the former French territories, particularly by Léopold Senghor, himself a distinguished poet and the President of Senegal. *Négritude* has been defined as the quality of being African. Senghor has written a great deal about it, and his views have been well summarized by Ezekiel Mphahlele of the University of Ibadan in Nigeria: ". . . Senghor finds a heightened sensibility and intensity of emotion as the African's principal psychic traits. These are supposed to spring from years of humid-tropical living and a pastoral or agricultural closeness to the soil and the rhythms of the seasons. Emotion, he claims, is at the heart of *négritude:* 'Emotion is Negro.'" Césaire's poem itself contains the "dynamic quality" of *négritude* because it is "a passionate outcry, a self-vindication, it has an intensity of style, of imagery; abstract ideas are given a concrete meaning."

Self-vindication is a factor on both sides; the European justified his presence in part on the grounds that the African had accomplished so little, while the African justified his lack of accomplishment on the grounds that the important thing was to have emotion and sensibility. The common denominator is a lack of accomplishment—the failure of the Africans to work out by themselves and for themselves an indigenous, highly developed culture. And this raises a series of questions. How far is the premise actually correct? To the extent that it is correct, how can the failure be accounted for? In their search for a distinctively African cultural identity, what assets can Africans find in their traditional arts and crafts?

AS for the first question, it should already be clear that the stereotype of the African as a simple savage, a person unaware and apparently incapable of complex forms of social organization or of an integrated view of life, is decidedly inaccurate. Traditional African society was organized, and indeed sometimes overorganized, on every level from the family all the way up to the kingdom. Moreover, in a good many of the kingdoms, social and political relationships and the general level of sophistication were at least roughly comparable to those in European society during the Middle Ages; in fact, the western Sudanic kingdoms developed such startling parallels as cavaliers on horseback who went questing for fame and glory, slew monsters and villains and rescued damsels, and whose brave deeds and chivalric demeanor were woven into song and story by troubadours.

Yet it is likewise true that even among the most advanced societies, with singularly few exceptions, the methods for developing a high civilization—a civilization such as that of ancient Egypt, on the same continent—were lacking. Sir Philip Mitchell's statement suffers from the familiar peril of generalization, and all manner of exceptions can be taken to it. Well before the Colonial era many African languages had a vocabulary for expressing numbers up to 1,000; in at least one language, the Twi, any number could be expressed. Some tribes had their own calendar systems. Some also had standards of weight—the Ashanti, for instance, measured gold dust by balancing it on scales against counterweights of inferior metal, usually brass; the counterweights, which were beautifully wrought in the forms of birds, fish, and other creatures, are now valued museum pieces. Many tribes had currencies of one sort or another, such as bars of twisted metal in Liberia, copper crosses from Katanga to the Congo, or strings of cowrie shells which were in circulation across the continent. Some people of the northern Sudan used plows. There are other exceptions, too, which will be noted here later.

Nevertheless, when all the cultural variations and exceptions are taken into account, the fact remains that in nearly all African societies a good many of the basic tools—from mathematics and alphabet to plow and wheel—of intellectual and physical attainment were unknown or else known in only rudimentary and fragmentary form.

MANY reasons have been advanced, none of them really very satisfactory and some of them nonsensical. The debilitating effect of Africa's climate is one—yet Africa has a variety of climates, including some stimulating ones. Again, slavery—but internal slavery was not a cultural handicap (as witness Greece and Rome), slave exports were not sizable until the 16th Century, and although undoubtedly the trade in its later phases caused important social disruptions and a great loss of human resources, most societies in the interior regions and most of the population were affected relatively little. The prevalence of dietary deficiency is a partial answer, but it leads one in circles. In addition to soil factors and climatic vagaries, inadequate diet was often the result of the African's primitive methods and his tradition-bound devotion to a few, usually starchy or otherwise limited, staple foods.

Another and considerable part of the answer lay in the horrendous list of diseases that ravaged and weakened the population: recurrent fatal epidemics of plague, typhus, smallpox, yellow fever, pneumonia; endemic disabling or debilitating diseases such as malaria, sleeping sickness and leprosy, and other worm, fungus and parasitic infestations.

EVEN today, sickness and pain are a normal part of the tribal African's life, from birth to death. If this is true now, when the worst of the epidemic diseases have been brought under control and many people have at least a rudimentary knowledge of hygiene, how much more hopeless life must have seemed, and how much more effort and prayer and magic and mental concentration must have been devoted to the thought of survival, in earlier times. As Sir Philip Mitchell notes, "In three or four years at the beginning of this century sleeping sickness killed 100,000 people in Uganda." And yet, of course, in weighing this factor, it must be remembered that disease existed in the same order of magnitude in other parts of the world; in India, China and Southeast Asia, which nevertheless became the sites of early, sophisticated cultures.

No doubt the answer lies in the complex interrelationship of many factors, some of which are likely to remain unknown. Quite certainly, however, despite the wishful rationalizations of racial bigots and numerous pseudoscientific efforts to the contrary, there is not even a grain of evidence for the notion that Africans are biologically inferior and have been designed by nature for an inferior role in the family of mankind. Anthropological studies indicate that they have the same range of intellectual capacities,

the same potentialities for responding to an intellectually enriching environment—in short, precisely the same amount of brain power—as all the other races and racial polyglots of the world, from Eskimos to the white settlers of South Africa.

This would seem to mean, by logical extension, that such concepts as *négritude* and "the African Personality" are in fact meaningless. However, equality in all the fundamental qualities of intellect—such as the ability to learn, the ability to solve problems, and so forth—does not preclude the possibility that subtle differences may exist and that they can be transmitted genetically as more or less characteristic ethnic attributes. Anthropology being an inexact science, and psychology an even less exact one (in spite of the scholarly paraphernalia with which each surrounds itself), such differences have never been demonstrated scientifically, let alone measured, to the satisfaction of anyone except the person who is doing the demonstrating and measuring.

In any case, since other peoples flatter themselves with their national or racial ethos, and since only the most narrow-minded behavioral psychologist would swear that the commonly observed temperamental differences among peoples are entirely the result of environment, the Africans are justified in hoping that they have special talents.

These qualities, traits, values, attitudes—inborn and/or conditioned—are manifested mainly in the African's art. The word is used in the broad sense as defined by Webster: "Application of skill and taste to production according to esthetic principles." To it should be added the proviso that the principles may be sensed rather than consciously formulated and that beauty always and everywhere lies in the eye of the beholder.

AFRICA'S traditional art includes something of every important form, even architecture. "Mud, poles, and thatch," as Sir Philip Mitchell indicates (and, he might have added, among some pastoralists, liberal amounts of cow dung mixed into the mud as a binder) are hardly the materials of great architecture. Yet the mud palaces of Kano, for instance, have a certain massive grace, and here and there in Africa one finds the poles and thatch handled with elegance. This is notably so in Buganda: the antechambers and mausoleums for the dead kings, with their reed wicker walls, their immaculate roofs of heavy thatch, their supporting poles wrapped in russet brown bark cloth, are certainly as moving both esthetically and spiritually in their own context as some of the well-regarded churches and shrines of Europe.

MOREOVER, although mud, poles and thatch (and animal skins and tree trunks and other such items easily available in a given locality) have been the customary materials, it is untrue that Africans "... had built nothing, nothing of any kind, in any material more durable." From Somalia and Ethiopia all the way to the Transvaal region in the Republic of South Africa, archaeologists have found the remains of towns, fortresses and castlelike structures built of stone. For a while it was generally assumed that these must have been the products of Arabic or other foreign influence, but now it is agreed that many—perhaps even all—were created by Africans.

Who these people were and what happened to destroy their culture are matters for speculation and perhaps always will be—for again, in spite of their technical skill, they left no written records except for a few, dim, so-far undeciphered hieroglyphs. Tentatively they are called "Azanians," on the assumption that they had some relationship to the people the earliest traders found living along the eastern coast, a region (from the Horn to Zanzibar) known to the early Mediterranean world by the Greek name, Azania. It seems likely that they had acquired some of their cultural traits, particularly their remarkable stonemasonry, as the result of migrations that took place from the Ethiopian plateau to the south (*Chapter 3*), since stonework of the same type was common there. In any case their skill was impressive, as

demonstrated especially at Zimbabwe in Southern Rhodesia.

Here is the greatest archaeological mystery of the whole continent: a complex of granite structures, stretching over hill and plain, including an elliptical-shaped building—a palace, or temple, or both—300 feet long and 220 feet wide, with walls 30 feet high and 20 feet thick. For a time this site was the capital of the Monomotapa, the great chiefs of the interior with whom the Portuguese of Mozambique negotiated in their attempts to discover "the gold of Ophir." But some of the ruins date back to far earlier times, perhaps as far back as the Sixth or Seventh Century A.D., while others seem to stem from a time as recent as the early 18th Century.

One early investigator concluded that the elliptical building was modeled on the palace in ancient Jerusalem where the Queen of Sheba stayed, and that another large structure on a hilltop was an attempted reproduction of King Solomon's temple on Mount Moriah in the Holy Land—a romantic thesis in view of the possible Ethiopian derivation of the construction techniques. But this is contradicted by other evidence, and so Zimbabwe remains an enigma—except in one regard. It was produced by Africans.

THERE is a lesser but also intriguing mystery about the rock paintings and engravings that have been found in many parts of Africa. Mostly of animals or of humans and animals in hunting scenes, often executed with delicacy and a refined sense of design and movement, they can be seen on cave walls and other protected rock faces from the Sahara all the way (except for the forest regions) to the Cape of Good Hope, and in chronology they range from a few hundred to thousands of years old. Presumably those in the north were done by Caucasoid peoples, but the evidence indicates that most of the others were the products of the Bushmen—who, as we saw earlier, formerly roamed great areas of east, central and southern Africa. If so (and there is no other feasible explanation), the Bushmen present one of history's most profound examples of cultural retrogression, for today their creative output is limited to a few very simple utensils and ornaments made of grass, strips of skin and ostrich-egg shells.

Although it has no written literature, Africa has a rich and varied heritage of "oral literature"—aphorisms and wise sayings beyond counting, proverbs, folktales, oral "history," legends and sagas, some of the latter as fully elaborated as the old Norse sagas such as Beowulf (which also of course were originally oral). Frequently the stories became songs: some tribes have scores and even hundreds of songs, varied enough to suit almost any occasion. Instrumental music was limited by lack of technology and materials; even so, musicians could achieve a surprising range of notes and tonal qualities from what they had, particularly from the numerous kinds of drums. One form of "talking drum," shaped like an hourglass and carried slung from the player's shoulder, is so versatile that it is used for telling stories and sending messages; in the hands of an expert, its sounds are poetry.

Both in music and dancing the African's gift for rhythm is so famous as to need no comment—except, perhaps, to say that the gift is as apparent in the native scene, whether it be a tribal rite in a forest clearing in Uganda or a citified dance hall in Ghana's Accra (source of the catchy, jazzy, free-wheeling dance music called "High Life") as it is among Africa's descendants in Harlem.

BY far the most highly developed of Africa's arts, however, is sculpture. It covers a wide range of materials and purposes. There are massive stone carvings at Zimbabwe, for instance; terra cotta figures at least a thousand years old have been found at Ife, in Yorubaland in southern Nigeria; ivory was used considerably, and sometimes also "hippo ivory"—from the tusks of that beast. At Ife and at Benin, the casting of bronze (by the cire-perdue or lost wax process) was brought to extraordinary technical perfec-

AFRICAN INFLUENCE on modern art showed up dramatically in Picasso's 1906-1907 *Les Demoiselles d'Avignon*, now owned by New York's Museum of Modern Art.

tion, and the Ashanti of the Gold Coast were equally adept in the use of gold. The predominant material, however, since it was so much more plentiful and so much easier to work, was wood.

As for the sculptors' purposes, they were as diverse as those that motivate sculptors anywhere: the esthetic satisfaction that the artist felt in creation, the esthetic pleasure that the customer felt in looking at the object. However, for the most part, both creation and use were intimately connected with African religious beliefs. The gold or ivory amulet was not merely an ornament but a device for warding off evil forces and attracting good ones. The sculptured figure of an ancestor was not merely something to remember him by; it was also a way to please his soul and secure his favor, and moreover, it could serve as the soul's temporary residence after its return to earth.

Similarly, the image of a god or spirit, when housed in a shrine or "spirit house" with suitable invocations, became its physical, visible extension and could be worshiped or supplicated or placated directly. The hunter, by means of ceremonial manipulations of an animal's image, could influence the behavior of the animal itself; a childless woman, by wearing a little doll-like representation of an infant, could conceive and have a child.

It has been the African's belief in the spiritual nature of reality, the indistinguishable merging of the visible and invisible, that mainly accounted for the distortions that so often characterized his art. The elongations and truncations, the disproportionate size of certain parts of the anatomy or of certain facial features, were not due to lack of technical skill or to any failure in perceiving how people and objects actually look. They were due rather to the artist's attempts to capture the *idea* of his subject, to present what was essential and meaningful about it—in short, his purpose was to summarize or "abstract" its total reality. Thus, through *négritude* as some would say, "abstract ideas are given a concrete reality."

MODERN European "abstract art" is to a very considerable degree an outgrowth of this ancient African concept. In the early 20th Century, following the recently established rule of European countries in Africa, many African art objects found their way to Paris. This was a time of effervescent experimentalism among many of the "school of Paris" painters, and the African creations caused considerable excitement among men such as Vlaminck, Matisse, Braque, Derain. The most excited was a young Spaniard, Pablo Picasso, who had been attracted by the semiabstract work of Cézanne and who found in the African sculptures the elements needed to trigger his own imagination.

The result, in 1906, was a painting called *Two Nudes*—two almost identically squat, thick, stylized females seen from different views—and, in 1907, the masterpiece of his "Negro period," a painting called *Les Demoiselles d'Avignon* in which both figure and background were "abstracted" into an arrangement of contending planes, lines and curves. The next stage was pure cubism, and the rest is history—European art history.

It is a peculiar irony that as European art has become more abstract, expressionistic and dynamic, African art has become progressively more sedate and unimaginative. Sculptures of the kind that thrilled Picasso, and that soon were being sought after by museums and collectors, very rarely are produced now. The relative decline in traditional religious beliefs, the weakening of tribal institutions, the tendency to absorb the white man's viewpoint—many reasons have been suggested. In any case, somehow the sap and vitality that nourished the masterpieces of the past are no longer present.

IT should be added that none of these art forms could properly be called characteristic of Tropical Africa. Artistic practices, products, and skills were immensely varied throughout the region. There are numerous stone ruins, but there is only one Zimbabwe. Sculpture was produced only in the basins of the Congo and the Niger, which take in only about a fourth of Tropical Africa, and even here a great many tribes practiced it little or badly. Among many of the nomadic pastoral peoples, art, far from being admired, was looked down on—the artisans who made necessary tools and objects (blacksmiths among the Masai, for instance) were considered inferiors of their fellow tribesmen and were segregated in a lower caste. By and large, art flourished only among sedentary peoples and under favorable conditions: one of these was a sufficient ease of livelihood to give time for leisure; the other was the existence of wealthy, appreciative patrons such as the kings and nobles of Ashanti, Bini and Bushongo.

But, of course, leisure and patronage have been the key factors in the development of the arts in almost all other parts of the world. And as Africa advances in the modern world—as general living standards are raised, as capital accumulates in government or private hands—these necessary conditions undoubtedly will spread and may bring a new and greater artistic flowering. Quite certainly, scattered within the African tradition, there are plenty of seeds for great accomplishments.

STOOL MAKER among the craftsmanlike Ashanti people (*left*) puts final touches to a decorative stool which he carved in a few days out of a single block of wood.

HAND WEAVER deftly maneuvers the shuttle of his ramshackle loom (*opposite*). To master the complex craft, Ashanti weavers begin their training in early childhood.

The Presence of Beauty in Useful Crafts

Art in Africa has never been a specialized activity cut off from other concerns. Traditionally, an African artist was first of all a craftsman fabricating useful objects, and often enough he made them beautiful. Whether his product was a mask carved for magical ritual, a piece of cloth woven for a ceremonial robe or a necklace fashioned to ward off evil, the artist in fulfilling a utilitarian purpose imbued his work with a beauty that has always been unmistakable.

PRANCING GIRL was painted by a Negro people before 5000 B.C. on a rock wall at Tassili-n-Ajjer, a once fertile area in the central Sahara.

LOPING CATTLE were fluently depicted around 4000 B.C. at Tassili-n-Ajjer. This and the picture shown above are copies made by experts.

SCULPTURED SANCTUARY formed of bricks and clay (*above*) by the Dogon people of Mali has the appearance of a huge piece of pottery.

MYSTERIOUS RUINS of Zimbabwe in Southern Rhodesia (*opposite*) are dominated by massive walls erected by an unknown African people.

SUN-BAKED STOREHOUSE for the sacred fetishes of the Dogon people (*left*) looks as if it had been shaped from the bleak desert ground.

MAGICAL SCULPTURE was created by men who believed their carvings embodied living spirits

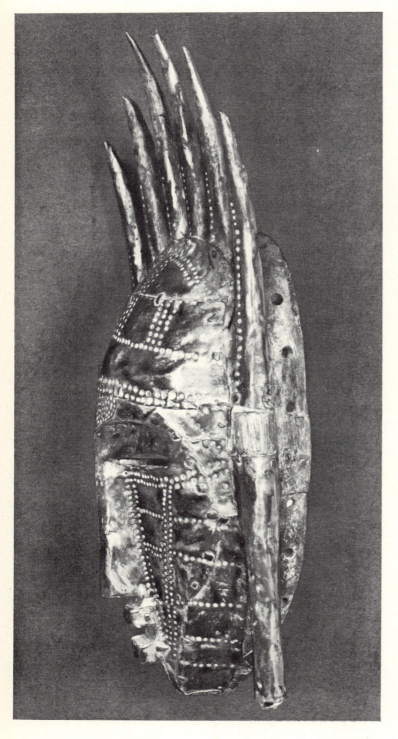

ANCESTOR STATUE was not intended merely to represent a man. To the west African who carved it, the figurine housed the ancestral spirit itself.

HORNED FETISH made of wood and plated with metal (*left*) is used as a mask in ritual dances. Most masks were designed to evoke fear and awe.

GHASTLY MASK carved with diagrammatic simplicity and painted a deathly white (*opposite*) is used in the rites of a west African secret society.

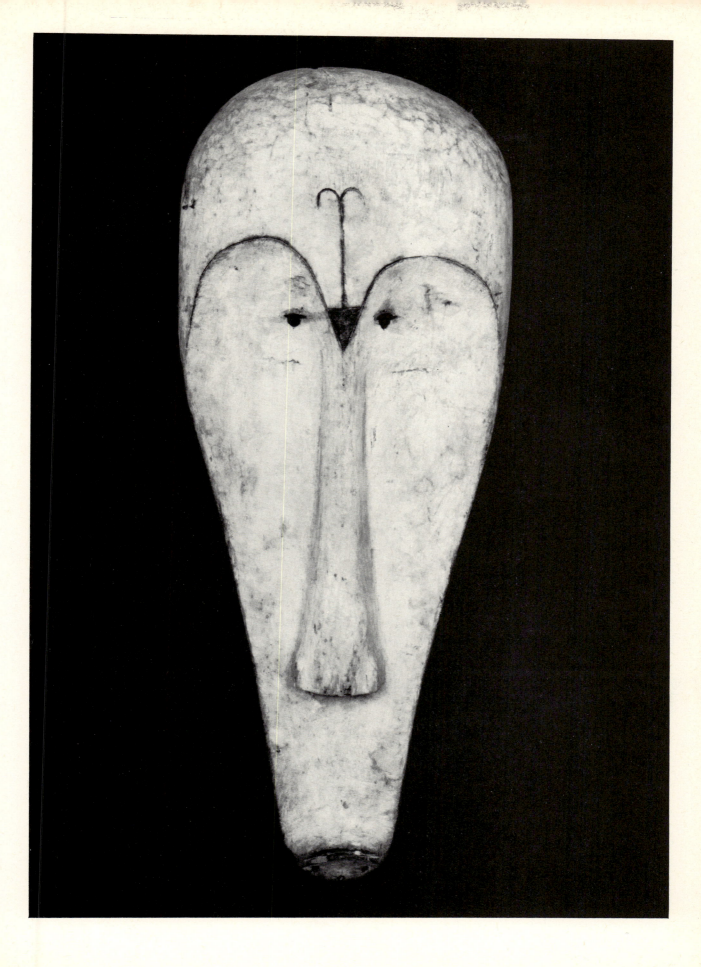

ROYAL VISIT by the Queen of England to Nigeria brings out crowds of robed Moslems and a gyrating array of dancers. Nigeria, acquired by Great Britain in the 19th Century, peacefully gained its independence in 1960.

8

Colonialism's Disputed Legacy

AFRICA, in a sense, is the oldest and the newest area of the world. The first manlike creature, as the Leakeys' discoveries indicated, may well have originated here millions of years ago. Yet it was not until the explorers and colonizers came to the African continent in the 19th Century that this mysterious area began to emerge from its obscurity.

Measured against Africa's long history, the colonial era was a mere episode lasting less than 100 years. But it was a decisive episode, one that quite literally shaped the political and the economic character of contemporary Africa in irreversible ways. In fact, it has given Africa a destiny which is no longer specifically African but which inevitably must reflect the influential presence (in Tropical Africa alone) of some 750,000 Europeans and 400,000 Asians, with *their* skin colors and cultures and aspirations. Pliny the Elder, the Roman naturalist, had marveled: "Always something new out of Africa." Colonialism brought something entirely new into Africa—and what comes out will again be something new.

Who were the "colonialists"? Why did they come? What did they want from Africa and the Africans? What were their methods? Before the irresistible forces of African nationalism caused

125

its sudden decline in the 1950s, what had colonialism accomplished?

These are large questions, and the answers to them not only involve many complex variables but obviously are also subject to different interpretations. Nevertheless, while keeping this in mind, there are some main points that can be dealt with briefly and (it is hoped) objectively.

THE most concise explanation for the 19th Century "opening up of Africa" is that Europeans had previously limited their attentions to the coast because their commercial interests lay there, particularly in the slave trade; and when slaving was outlawed, and the Industrial Revolution put the Europeans in need of raw materials and of markets for their manufactured goods, they went inland for the good of their pocketbooks.

This idea, summed up in the word "imperialism," is a favorite property of Marxists—among whom one would include a number of today's African nationalist leaders. And it contains a great deal of truth. But, like all such exercises in historical shorthand, it overlooks much, and what is overlooked here is that Europe's main interests in Africa during most of the 19th Century were nonexploitive. Often they were worthy, in some cases admirable.

Sierra Leone, a west African country somewhat bigger than West Virginia in size and population, and since 1961 an independent self-governing member of the British Commonwealth, owes its existence to a humanitarian concern. It came into being because British Abolitionists in 1787 purchased land there for the resettlement of liberated slaves. (The capital of Sierra Leone appropriately is named Freetown.) Subsequently in 1821 an abolitionist group in the U.S., called the American Colonization Society, acting on an idea of Thomas Jefferson's and with the encouragement of President Monroe, secured an adjoining area for the resettlement of slaves freed in America. In 1847 this became the Republic of Liberia (in Latin, "Land of Freedom"), the second-oldest independent nation—the first being Ethiopia

—of today's Tropical Africa and the only one with an unbroken record of independence.

This same revulsion against slavery had much to do with the discovery of what lay within Africa's interior, and with the establishment of European authority there. For, in spite of international agreements against the export of slaves in the early 19th Century and despite British naval patrols to enforce the prohibition, Arab slavers in east Africa continued the commerce in devious ways. Since it could not be stopped effectively at the shoreline, where the small Arab dhows could slip in at night at innumerable spots, load and be gone, the conviction grew that the only practical way to stop it was at its sources in the interior. Christian missionary-explorers were mainly responsible, especially the great Dr. David Livingstone. It was they who denounced the situation and created public demands in Europe that it end; it was Livingstone who found the main slaving depots, which by mid-century lay far back from the coast; and it was Livingstone who, directly or by inference, promulgated the belief that there was no remedy short of forceful intervention and the establishment inside Africa of European standards of law and order.

ALONG with the missionaries, another group was responsible for Africa's opening: the fact-finders. Their sponsors were various and their motives were mixed, but by and large they represented the spirit of inquiry, the cerebral itch that makes humans value knowledge for its own sake. What was it like in Timbuktu? To a Frenchman named René Caillié the question seemed so important that he spent four years preparing to find out; disguised as an Arab, he reached the old city at last in 1828. Henry Morton Stanley was in the same tradition, really: he was an American journalist who came to Africa on an assignment for the New York *Herald* (". . . start looking around for Livingstone," his editor had said. "If he is dead, bring every possible proof"), and was so stimulated by the challenge of the unknown that in time he became one of the greatest explorers, discovering the Congo basin (Stanleyville is named for him) and exploring a great deal more of central Africa.

Between them, the fact-finders and the missionaries, by arousing the European public's interest and its righteous concern, prepared the emotional basis for Europe's involvement.

IN the latter part of the 19th Century, the great European powers were engaged in a fierce political and economic rivalry. Colonies were eagerly sought after for the prestige that they implied in this struggle. Industrialization created a growing demand for raw materials; progress in engineering and medical science reduced the hazards of colonizing the African interior. European businessmen and political leaders began to realize, as Sir Philip Mitchell has said, that the new lands offered possibilities for "valuable trade and substantial profits, provided, however, that stable and humane governments were established, a task which had defeated the peoples of the region almost completely. . . ." Investment groups had begun to form; the great powers eyed one another suspiciously and jockeyed for position. Suddenly, the "scramble for Africa" had begun.

And truly it was a scramble: a time of chaos and wild incongruity, a melee of governments and privately owned "chartered companies"; a time when, in Mitchell's words, "it was an almost casual business to acquire by private enterprise a central African possession as large as many of the larger countries of Europe." Indeed, as Stanley demonstrated, it was possible to acquire an area that was four times the size of France. Arriving in Europe in 1878 after his epic voyage of discovery down the Congo River, he was hired by Belgium's King Leopold II to go back and secure for him and his financial backers—not for Belgium—territorial concessions in the Congo basin. In five years of negotiating with the native chiefs Stanley accomplished this mission.

A semblance of order was attained at a conference held in Berlin in 1884-1885 to try to establish rules for the colonial game: in the future land was supposed to be actually occupied in order to be legitimately claimed. Another result was that the Congo was recognized as a sovereign state under the suzerainty (in effect, the personal ownership) of Leopold, who thus became sovereign of the "Congo Free State" in addition to being king of Belgium. But much was left unsettled, and England, Germany, France, Italy and Portugal continued maneuvering to expand their "spheres of influence in Africa."

Portugal yearned to unite Angola and Mozambique by acquiring the central region between, and hardly a year after the conference it made moves to do so, only to have them frustrated by the efforts principally of one man, Cecil Rhodes. As the leading developer of south Africa's diamond and gold fields, Rhodes had become immensely rich and powerful; and he wanted the region for England as part of his dream of extending British rule from the Cape to Cairo. After maneuvering Britain into acquiring Bechuanaland in 1885, Rhodes three years later secured effective control over most of what is now Southern Rhodesia by persuading Lobengula, the paramount chief of the area, to sign a treaty by which he surrendered all mining rights in the area.

BY 1891, largely through Cecil Rhodes's manipulations, British "protection" extended over a large part of the region that became known as Northern Rhodesia and Nyasaland. On the other hand, England coveted Madagascar, which was under French "influence," and did not formally give up its claim in favor of the French until that same year. Similarly Germany, with all of Tanganyika, coveted the island of Zanzibar and the strip of coastal territory owned by the Sultan on the mainland opposite. It also had designs on Tanganyika's northern neighbor, Uganda. In 1890, part of the strip was sold to Germany by the Sultan (the rest was later leased by the British for use by Kenya). Germany forswore her claims to Zanzibar and Uganda; England gave Germany the island of Helgoland in the North Sea (which it then converted into a fortress for its fight against England in World War I).

By the opening of this century, however, the dismemberment was virtually complete and reasonably neat. There were no major changes until after World War I, when the German colonies—Tanganyika, Ruanda-Urundi, the Cameroons and Togoland—were taken from it and put under the protection of the League of Nations, which parceled them out to the victors to administer under League supervision. After World War II these League mandates became United Nations trust territories. In this way Tanganyika, part of Togoland and part of the Cameroons were assigned to Britain, the other parts of Togoland and the Cameroons went to France, and Ruanda-Urundi to Belgium.

IT may seem strange that all this failed to provoke general revolt among the Africans at the time it was happening. The answer is that the African masses had hardly a clue as to what was going on; neither, in most cases, did their leaders. Stanley did not "conquer" the Congo. He made treaties with native rulers by which he promised trade goods or "protection" in return for the cooperation of the unwitting chiefs —and their peoples. To the west, across the Congo and Ubangi Rivers, Count Savorgnan de Brazza was doing the same for France.

Only occasionally did the colonial powers have to use force to achieve their aims. In Guinea the French encountered an intractable chief named Samory, who led a guerrilla war against them for 16 years before he was captured and exiled. (Sékou Touré, his grandson, became the Republic of Guinea's first president in 1958.) The British invaded and conquered the Kingdom of Benin, part of present Nigeria, in 1897, and were met by vast numbers of corpses, slaughtered in ritual offerings to the Bini gods. In the Gold Coast—now Ghana—the Kingdom of Ashanti put up fierce resistance, submitting to the British only after a long series of wars. There were other wars, notably against the Kingdom of Dahomey in West Africa, the Matabele in Southern Rhodesia and the Xhosa,

Zulu, Bechuana and Basuto in southern Africa. Yet, in the main, especially considering the hugeness of the area and the multitude of rulers and tribes, the process of extending the colonial domain was extraordinarily peaceful.

It was also extraordinarily inept and short-sighted. Leaving aside moral issues for the moment, the most striking aspect of the whole scene was its quality of inadvertence—not European cunning but European dreadful ignorance. The explorers had found the mountains and knew how the rivers ran, and the missionaries and explorers together had taken rough readings on African life, but there was no comprehension of Africa's complexities. Hence, when the boundaries were drawn, they often made no sense geographically, economically, culturally or ethnically.

Peoples who disliked one another often were lumped together. Conversely, tribes and ethnic groups were fragmented. The Somalis were divided five ways: there were British, French and Italian Somalilands, plus a Somali enclave in Kenya and another in Ethiopia. The Bakongo tribe, with its strong sense of community derived from the old Kingdom of Kongo, was separated by the borders of the Belgian Congo, Portuguese Angola and the French territory of the Middle Congo.

THE latter exemplified another aspect of the same arbitrariness and myopia. For administrative convenience, France divided its major sub-Saharan holdings into two units, French West Africa and French Equatorial Africa, with capitals respectively at Dakar and Brazzaville; these in turn, for further convenience, were chopped into territories—eight of them in the first instance, four in the second (the Middle Congo being one of these)—with little awareness or concern as to whether the boundaries intersected tribal and ethnic groupings, and with no idea that they might someday be the national borders of independent countries.

In short, the "scramble for Africa" left the map of modern Africa—scrambled. The sizes and shapes and components of the new nations today are irrational: they are simply the accidental debris left behind after the dissolution of a historical interlude. The result is that their internal relationships and their relationships with one another are as mixed up and unstable as an underdone omelet.

This is one of colonialism's legacies to Africa. In political terms, it is probably the most important one. There are, of course, a variety of others—their variety stemming from the cardinal fact that there was not "a" European colonial policy but as many policies as colonial powers. Moreover, these policies evolved piecemeal. Their purposes changed as circumstances changed—and even when aims were fixed, the practical applications were often inconsistent. However, after the dust had begun to settle, certain general patterns did emerge. It behooves us to see what they were, or professed to be, in the cases of the four main powers. Then the results can be compared.

FIRST, what did they have in common? All of the colonial powers left a measure of western technology and culture and a crude sense of territorial identity. More specifically, they left such legacies as common languages, a framework of administration and at least the beginnings of territory-wide economies, transport and communications systems and the development of natural resources and scientific agricultural methods. The main theme of colonial expansion was material advantage—cheap and dependable sources of raw materials, new markets for manufactured goods. The instruments were those of private enterprise, mainly big chartered companies, since large amounts of capital were required to develop the resources under the primitive and difficult conditions that prevailed. One of the biggest attractions in central and southern Africa was mining: enormous investments went into the mines and into the facilities—roads, railways, ports—needed to get their output to market. These large projects needed large supplies of workers, and so there began the drift of Africans away from their villages and tribal areas to the mines and towns,

and with this a slow weakening of the old, traditional values of African life.

The development of plantations—for palm oil, cocoa, coffee, rubber and other tropical produce—also was likely to be a costly business. To safeguard this growing economic apparatus, and to insure stability and order, the various colonial governments had to supply a growing officialdom. Thus, although the number of Europeans in Africa steadily increased and their functions broadened and some became deeply entrenched as landowners and as businessmen, their roles were largely those of administrators, managers and technicians. As nearly as possible, they lived a European life amid cultural and physical appurtenances duplicated from their European homelands. It was not that they lacked interest in Africa. But their main interest was in seeing that all this machinery (a category in which they frequently tended to include the Africans) continued to work properly.

A second and somewhat contrasting common theme, to which the colonial nations gave much more prominent display, was that they had a "civilizing mission" in Africa. They had a moral duty to lift the African from his ignorance and poverty—his "state of social degradation" as the Portuguese Colonial Charter, which is still in effect, terms it—and lead him toward the benefits that history had somehow denied him. As to how this should be done, however, and at what pace, and what "civilized" attributes should be emphasized, there were differences of opinion. The attitudes of the principal colonial powers have been summed up under the labels of Belgian Paternalism, French Identity, Portuguese Assimilation and British Empiricism.

BELGIAN Paternalism did not emerge until after 1908, when Leopold officially handed over the Congo to the Belgian state. His own policy, while professing a desire to help the Africans, had essentially been that of an absentee landlord interested in making as big a profit as possible from his estate. He never visited the

Congo; he let it out to his own agents and concessionaires, kept a close eye on their accounts and grumbled whenever dividends did not measure up to his expectations. As a result, there was widespread use of forced labor and atrocious punishments (workers who displeased their bosses often had their right hands cut off). These scandals caused such an uproar that Leopold was compelled to appoint a commission of inquiry, and subsequently the Belgian government annexed the Congo. Leopold's regime is believed to have cost some five to eight million lives. The government's policy thereafter, as Lord Hailey, the British colonial expert, has said, was marked by a "general determination that . . . rule of the colony should be such as to present the strongest possible contrast to the history of the Free State under Leopold II."

The central concept on which this policy operated was that the Congolese were still in the childhood stage of human development; their growth to responsible adulthood required time, patience and carefully ordered progress from one phase to the next, in wholesome surroundings and under the benevolent but firm guidance provided by the wise Belgian parent. They had their duties, their place and their rights, but for a long time to come there could be no thought of training them for self-government; children do not vote. For that matter nobody, black or white, not even most Belgians living in the Congo, had any political rights. Meanwhile, as the colony's prosperity grew, the native Congolese would be supplied with more and more of the things that were good for them—clinics and other health services, schools, churches, housing, recreation—and, being intelligent children, they would be grateful.

French Identity was based on the principle of a French Revolutionary decree of 1792 that

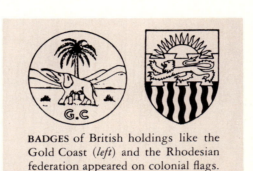

BADGES of British holdings like the Gold Coast (*left*) and the Rhodesian federation appeared on colonial flags.

"all men, without distinction of color, domiciled in French colonies, are French citizens, and enjoy all the rights assured by the Constitution." To be sure, it took a while for the principle to be put into effect, and meanwhile French rule was largely authoritarian, involving such unseemly episodes as military conquest, forced labor and hardfisted suppression of individual rights. But in the end the ideas of *liberté, égalité, fraternité* prevailed. In 1946 France and all its territories, African and otherwise, became part of the French Union, whose inhabitants from that day were Frenchmen with a single, all-encompassing identity. The executive authority continued to be centralized in France, but Frenchmen overseas were represented in the Assembly of the French Union and in parliament. Within this theoretical framework, France saw its mission as that of enabling the colored Frenchmen—by educating as many of them as possible and as quickly as possible with the means available—to become responsible and intelligent citizens.

Portuguese Assimilation had its origin in an even more radically egalitarian theory. Not only were the African territories considered to be integral parts of Portugal and their inhabitants to be Portuguese, and not only was the goal that of creating "a complete moral, political, and economic unity," but miscegenation was to be encouraged. The way to get rid of racial misunderstandings, in the Portuguese view (and the logic is unassailable), was to get rid of races. The ultimate aim, in theory at least, was racial assimilation, the emergence of a mulatto population.

This policy of Assimilation is still in effect. As one Portuguese Minister of Colonies has remarked: "In diffusing our blood, our language and our religion, our only purpose was that high aim of making others equal to us. . . ."

The measure of equality was that the African be literate in Portuguese, accept Christianity, put aside tribal loyalties and native customs, prove that he was of good character and earned enough to support himself and his family, and in general behave and think like a Portuguese. At that point he was considered assimilated and acquired full Portuguese citizenship.

MEANTIME, however, he remained an *indígena*, or native. He lived under a separate code of laws and was subjected to numerous rules and prohibitions appropriate to his inferior status. Most important, he was subject to forced labor, the widespread use of which has been condoned by Portuguese authorities. Able-bodied *indígenas* in Mozambique were compelled by law to work for an employer six months out of the year unless they could prove that they had already done the necessary quota of work on their own land, if they had any. One official has said in defense of the system, ". . . it is nonsense to treat all Africans alike. The only thing they have in common is color."

There was little hope that the African could in fact become assimilated. The attainment of a high school education and a decent wage—both basic requirements for assimilation—was practically impossible. Furthermore, the system created a gulf between the few qualified Africans and their countrymen who were not so fortunate, and thus—it was hoped—served to cut off nationalism at the source. According to a Portuguese census taken in 1950, there were roughly 34,000 *assimilados* and 51,000 mulattoes (who automatically were full citizens) out of a total population in Angola and Mozambique numbering 9,700,000. In other words, less than 1 per cent of the Africans were *assimilados* or mulattoes with full Portuguese citizenship, and the rest—except the 141,000 Europeans—were *indígenas* with status as Portuguese "nationals" who enjoyed none of the rights of citizenship.

British Empiricism, as the term implies, has been a matter of cut-and-try and learning (if sometimes slowly) from experience. It has been called "resilient" and "flexible," and, less kindly, "incoherent," "opportunistic" and "a succession of uncoordinated responses to different types of stimulus." It grew from the facts that Britain's territorial interests in Africa had been acquired as much by accident as design, that they lay scattered all over the map and were all sizes and shapes and contained all manner of people and geography, and that they had been brought into the fold under a variety of legal arrangements which ranged from outright arbitrary annexation to leasing. Seeing no virtue in consistency for its own sake, the British adapted their policies to the particular circumstances.

As a result, British Africa came into the present era with all sorts of social and political patterns—notably (and agonizingly, as it would prove) in regard to white settlement. In some places, such as Nigeria, the Gold Coast and Uganda, Europeans were not allowed to own land—in the words of Lord Lugard, a famous British governor of Nigeria, "the land was the property of the people, held in trust for them by their chiefs." In other places, such as Nyasaland, white settlement on a long-term, landowning basis was allowed but not encouraged. In still others, such as the Rhodesias and Kenya, it was actively encouraged.

NEVERTHELESS, as time went on, British policy did develop an underlying theme of great importance. It was the idea that sooner or later the colonial areas would become independent, or at any rate internally autonomous, and that Britain accordingly had a responsibility to train the peoples living there to run their own affairs successfully. So there would have to be schools—and ways for the most promising students to go on to the universities. There would have to be (within limits) freedom of speech and of the press, and freedom to organize political parties and trade unions. There would have to be a growing participation by Africans in the apparatus of the territorial governments. The pace was leisurely, funds were limited, inconsistencies were rampant and the road was bumpy, but it would lead—so it was hoped—to "responsible self-government within the Commonwealth in conditions that ensure to the people both a fair standard of living and freedom from oppression. . . ."

This enlightened policy was practical in terms of Britain's interests. By helping its territories, especially those in west Africa, to achieve independence, Britain also hoped to retain their friendship and its own favorable economic position. Britain expected its territories to show proof of economic viability, and especially in white settler areas it expected them to protect the interests of all resident communities.

By the early 1950s, as the colonial era was drawing to a close, these four policies had led to four rather distinct sets of results in education, economics and political development.

In education, the Portuguese Africans were at the bottom of the ladder, being almost entirely illiterate. The Congolese had the highest degree of literacy among adults (35 to 40 per cent) in Tropical Africa—but most had not gone beyond an elementary level. Few had had as much as a high school education, and scarcely any had had university training. In French and British areas adult illiteracy was massive, averaging close to 90 per cent; probably no more than 30 per cent of the people could read even in the most "advanced" places like Uganda and Madagascar. But an "educated elite" was fast emerging. Colleges had been established in Africa, and students were going on for advanced courses at universities in Britain and France. By 1950, French African students in European universities numbered 1,250; British African students, 3,500.

FROM an economic standpoint, the Congolese led the way. African laborers there had the highest standard of living—a result not only of Belgian policy but of the fact that the Congo, with its great mineral resources centered in Katanga, could afford social services and a relatively high wage scale. Here also was the highest degree of detribalization. In 1900 not one Congolese African lived outside his own tribal area, but by the 1950s more than three million did.

The Portuguese Africans were the least detribalized and their living standards were among the lowest. British and French areas were exceedingly patchy, with pockets of prosperity where development had occurred—the mining region of Northern Rhodesia, for instance, and the plantations of the Gold Coast and Ivory Coast. In such places an African middle class existed; elsewhere, life had scarcely changed, and bare subsistence was the rule.

POLITICAL progress was close to nil in Portuguese Africa. In the Congo, even by the mid-1950s, there was no vote and no effective participation by Africans in government: a great many worked for the colonial administration, but only in minor and usually routine jobs. In French territories the lower ranks of the civil service had been almost completely "Africanized," about half the middle ranks—bookkeepers, secretaries, etc.—had been, and about 15 per cent of the higher ranks. Moreover, not only were there well-organized political parties, but their elected representatives sat in the French parliament and several had risen to cabinet level in the French government.

In the British territories there was, of course, much variation politically, but except in the "white settler" areas—notably in Kenya and Southern Rhodesia—great progress had been made in Africanizing the civil service; Africans were substantially represented in both the executive and legislative branches of the various colonial governments; and in a few cases—notably the Gold Coast and Nigeria—they held a large majority of the seats in the legislature and in effect had achieved internal autonomy.

Thus the "colonial era" wore many faces and had many diverse effects. But, to the extent that the colonialists took their "civilizing mission" seriously, they had sown the seeds that would destroy the whole colonial system. And these seeds sprouted and grew in a riotous profusion that few, even as late as the mid-1950s, would have thought possible.

In the British protectorate of Zanzibar, a squad of the crack British-trained King's African Rifles stands ready for inspection.

The Modern Fruits of Fading Empires

The influence of the West is spreading in Africa, though colonialism itself is dying. Modern life is westernized life, and the manifold signs of contemporary civilization now lodged piece-meal in Africa—sidewalk cafés and parliaments, cash wages and disciplined armies, political parties and universities—are inevitably derived from western models. But inevitably, too, the ways of the West will assume new shapes as they merge with Africa's own varied heritage.

INDUSTRY, developed originally for the benefit of Europeans, has created new sources of wealth for Africans

CHUNKS OF COPPER are piled up at Elisabethville (*left*), the Congo city which lies in the heart of one of the world's richest mineral areas. Ore extraction has stimulated the growth of hundreds of subsidiary industries.

BATCH OF LOGS hewn from the rain forests of Ghana (*opposite*) is labeled for export. With Britain as a market for the bulk of the production, lumbering has become a sizable industry in both Ghana and Nigeria.

CARLOAD OF COAL is readied for dumping into a furnace (*left*) at the Rhodesian Iron and Steel Company in Southern Rhodesia. Although steel output is modest in Tropical Africa, there was none at all as late as 1943.

HIGHER EDUCATION is available

GOWNED FACULTY files past the modern campus bell tower (*left*) during graduation exercises at University College in Ibadan, Nigeria, an institution founded in 1947.

to very few as yet, but a tradition of academic learning has been solidly implanted

STUDENT NURSES in bright uniforms stroll outside Nigeria's 500-bed university hospital, built in 1954 as part of University College. In addition to nurses and mid-wives, some 180 medical students are trained here each year. The college, which has an enrollment of more than 1,000, is an affiliate of the University of London.

STREET CAFÉ in Leopoldville is part of the comfortable European city Belgian settlers built (*above*) largely for their own use in the heart of the Congo capital. Today, with independence, the European sector is being shared with the Congo's new middle class, a group composed mainly of skilled workers and government officials.

PIONEER TELEVISION built under British auspices in Nigeria features local talent whenever possible (*above*), but reruns of Hollywood movies are a popular staple.

PLUSH LOUNGE in Nairobi is frequented mainly by Europeans (*right*), who maintain their social isolation despite Britain's plan to make Kenya a multiracial society.

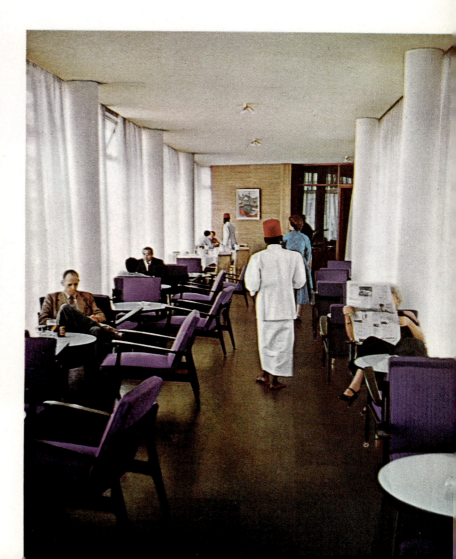

TRAINING in self-rule for nations-to-be was systematically offered by some colonial powers and just as systematically neglected by others

IN ORDERLY NIGERIA, parliament is opened by a procession of officials (*opposite*) bewigged in the English manner. In anticipation of independence, the British gave Nigerians key positions in the colonial government.

IN THE CHAOTIC CONGO, a villager casts a ballot at a jungle polling station (*right*) as Belgium gives the Congolese their first nationwide chance to vote—only six months before the Congo was granted its independence.

In Leopoldville, members of the powerful, tribe-based ABAKO party parade in protest against the late Patrice Lumumba, whose

anti-tribal sentiments and political policies they bitterly detested.

The Surge

to

Independence

THERE has been nothing in modern history like the past decade in Africa. At the end of 1955 there were only two independent nations in Tropical Africa—Ethiopia and Liberia. Seven years later there were 24, with several more candidates in various degrees of readiness waiting in the wings. By that time, too, the Congo had exploded. Civil war had come to Angola. Violent disturbances rumbled through the Central African Federation of Southern Rhodesia, Northern Rhodesia and Nyasaland. There was a violent upheaval in Ruanda. Among the new nations, political alliances, blocs and groups had formed, unformed and changed form in dizzying profusion. Leaders rose and fell. Here was history in the making, but history so fluid that what had seemed reasonably certain at a given point in time could be wholly outdated weeks or even days later.

With the dust still flying it is hard to trace cause-and-effect with any precision, and obviously impossible to predict what will happen next. Nevertheless, disarrayed and often baffling though the present scene is, it does contain patterns. The colonial "scramble" had its own dynamics, and so has the African Revolution. It didn't "just happen." It was caused. Since the circumstances differed from one territory to the next, the Revolution's course has varied correspondingly. Before noting these particulars, it will be useful to look at some general factors that underlie the whole African independence movement.

PERHAPS the most basic has been racial discrimination. Theoretically it did not exist in most parts of colonial Africa, but tacitly and effectively it did, to some degree, in almost every part. Socially it was demonstrated in innumerable ways, from a nuance of speech or attitude on the part of a Portuguese toward his supposedly assimilated African compatriot to the customary division of the new towns into European and African residential sections. Economically it was a good deal more tangible. Thomas Hodgkin, the eminent Oxford authority on African nationalism, could report as late as 1956 that, "Perhaps the most constant factor in the African industrial situation is the division between white employers and black workers. This situation is by no means confined to recognizably color bar countries. Those who are trained as engineers in France have difficulty in finding employment in French West Africa, on account of the unwillingness of most directors of firms to appoint Africans to posts in which they will be in a position to give orders to Europeans." Even when an African managed to rise to the same professional status as the European, he very often was paid at a lower rate.

There were the notable exceptions: the *évolués*, or culturally assimilated Africans, like Léopold Senghor, the poet-professor-politician from Dakar, who found themselves not only accepted but sometimes lionized in the salons of Paris, and the British West African intelligentsia, products of the best English universities, who consorted with the English officials and businessmen in their countries on terms of equality. But it was largely true that the African was made to feel inferior—and that he did not like it. When he was disdained, ordered about and treated as a mere commodity —as happened all too often—resentment turned to rancor and to thoughts of revenge.

Along with this, there was the African's growing discovery that "white superiority" was a myth—and furthermore a sinful one directly contradicted by the white man's own religion. These revelations came primarily through the work of the Christian missionaries. It was they who had set up the first schools, opening the way to literacy and knowledge, stimulating the appetite that led so many of today's African elite abroad for university training. Moreover, under the circumstances, the Bible could be hardly less than a revolutionary tract, especially the New Testament teachings about the brotherhood of men, their equality in the eyes of God, and the imminence of the end of the world when all earthly authority would be swept away and all men judged on their merits.

IN the hands of semiliterate converts, both the New and the Old Testaments furnished material for syncretic sects: sects combining the beliefs of African traditional religion with those taken from the new faith. Ideas emerged such as that in Heaven there would be a reversed color bar, only black men being admitted; that at the "second coming" Christ would manifest Himself as a black man. Numerous "prophets" appeared, and a frequent theme of their revelations was that the Kingdom of God could not be established until the white man had been driven from Africa. Resulting disturbances led to European suppressions which led to more disturbances. By 1952, there were more than 3,800 political prisoners in the Belgian Congo, most of them members of prophetic, anti-white sects.

The New World contributed both to the awakening and to the bizarre reactions that sometimes transpired. American missionaries came in droves, and largely through their efforts African students began arriving at U.S.

colleges—often to encounter American racism, but also to discover the revolutionary American principles of political democracy. Kwame Nkrumah (now president of Ghana), Nnamdi Azikiwe (now Governor General of Nigeria) and Dr. Hastings Banda (now chief minister of Nyasaland) were among the graduates. Less constructively, missionaries from the American sects such as the Jehovah's Witnesses spread apocalyptic doctrines which led to the above-mentioned prophets and visions.

There were important influences, too, from American Negro organizations. In 1910 the National Association for the Advancement of Colored People came into being with the objective of advancing not only colored citizens of the U.S. but colored people generally. As William Du Bois, one of its organizers, later wrote: "Most men in the world are colored. A belief in humanity means a belief in colored men. The future world will, in all reasonable possibility, be what colored men make it." The Universal Negro Improvement Association, founded in 1914 in Jamaica by Marcus Garvey and soon transplanted to New York, had an ambitious program: the development of unity among all the Negro peoples of the world, of an African Orthodox Church free of white influences, and of independent African nations which would, in turn, coalesce into a superstate, a United States of Africa.

GARVEY made his motto "Wake Up, Africa!", described himself as "Provisional President-General of Africa" and went so far as to create titles of nobility in the great nation-to-be and bestow them on his supporters. Fired by the spirit of "Garveyism," and responding to the writing and organizing work of Du Bois, Africans and people of African descent began holding Pan-African Congresses to discuss their problems and plans and to dream of the great, new, unified Africa.

These sessions were vital and so were the continuing discussions that went on among Africans abroad. There were émigrés like Dr. Hastings Banda, who had become a London physician. There were the parliamentarians and officials from French Africa, whose numbers grew as France implemented its policy of "identity." Above all there were the students. In Britain, a West African Students' Union had been formed by the mid-1920s. At its meetings, and in informal groups, ideas for "positive action" evolved. Jomo Kenyatta, Banda, Nkrumah and a number of other future movers and shakers in the nationalist movement met one another and plotted against "imperialism" at these gatherings which were held in London, the heart of the British Empire.

WORLD WAR II added important new elements to this already fermenting mixture. The defeats of Belgium and France and the early disasters suffered by Britain shattered the "image of authority" in their respective African territories and raised all manner of doubts among the subject peoples, while the Atlantic Charter, with its advocacy of "the right of all peoples to choose the form of government under which they will live," was taken by literate Africans to be a direct pledge of freedom. The rapid dissolution of colonialism in Asia was interpreted by African leaders to mean that the process should and could be extended to their continent. From the United Nations came both moral and political support. The General Assembly was a public forum for anti-colonialism, and the Trusteeship Council, taking over supervision of the old League of Nations mandated territories, pressed the responsible powers to fulfill their commitments (largely theoretical under the League) to prepare the African areas for self-government.

Thus in the decade after the war the situation grew increasingly volatile. As events were to show, only a few sparks were needed to touch it off. Sequences are necessarily somewhat blurred, but probably the single most incendiary factor was the proclaiming of independence for the Gold Coast—the new Ghana. The prime mover was Kwame Nkrumah, who became Ghana's president. His career has embodied so many of the elements of African nationalism—and may portend so much about the course of future developments in the new nations—that it is worth summarizing here.

Nkrumah was born in 1909 into what is still largely a tribal society, that of the Nzima, who are fishermen and agriculturists in the southwest corner of the Gold Coast. His father was a goldsmith with several wives and numerous children. Nkrumah's education began at local Catholic mission schools, and from there he went to a college established by the British for bright students. He came to the U.S. in 1935 and took a degree in economics and sociology at Lincoln University near Oxford, Pennsylvania, and an M.A. in philosophy at the University of Pennsylvania.

Along the way Nkrumah acquired a thorough grounding in African history and the literature of the African independence movement—especially the works of Marcus Garvey—and settled upon the goals of his life: liberation of the African territories, followed by Pan-African unity. He also decided on his methods: to organize the African people at the village level and mold them into political action machines that would demand independence, fight for it with strikes and boycotts—everything short of revolution.

FROM the U.S. Nkrumah went to London, where he studied law and became deeply involved in students' movements to promote African self-government. Back in Ghana, he organized a grass-roots Convention People's Party in 1949 and acquired a valuable asset when the British jailed him for his political activities, making him a martyr in the eyes of his fellow Africans. While he was still in jail his C.P.P. apparatus won the first general election in the Gold Coast, whereupon he was released so that he could, as head of the majority in the colony's Legislative Assembly, hold the office of Leader of Government Business.

From that moment onward the most urgent item of Government Business to Nkrumah and his associates was, naturally, the speeding up of independence. British empiricism accommodated itself to the facts. The transition period

lasted only six years. On March 6, 1957, the Gold Coast became the Republic of Ghana.

The celebrations there went on for a fortnight. The echoes, however, lasted for a long time, rebounding all over Africa, stirring the imaginations and quickening the pulses of the educated elite in all the other territories. They were relayed to remote and illiterate villagers to whom the terms "Ghana" and "nation" meant nothing, but who realized that somewhere men like themselves had acquired a desirable something called Independence. The fuse was lit; a chain reaction was about to begin.

BY French logic, the French African territories should have been little affected. Beginning in 1944, when General de Gaulle had met with African leaders at Brazzaville to work out postwar relationships, there had been a series of liberalizing and increasingly democratic French colonial measures, culminating in 1956 when the Socialist government of Guy Mollet produced a famous instrument known as the *loi-cadre*. It granted universal adult male and female suffrage, giving the forest Pygmy the same voting status as the graduate engineer living in Dakar or Brazzaville. The territories received effective control over their internal affairs. Meanwhile France also had begun a great program of public works and economic development, pouring money into its colonies at the rate of about $200 million a year. These steps were undertaken with the participation and approval of the African leaders, notably the Ivory Coast's Félix Houphouët-Boigny, co-founder and leader of the Rassemblement Démocratique Africain (R.D.A.) political party, which held a majority in most of the territories.

Nevertheless, certain inequities remained. *Liberté, egalité* and *fraternité* were still aims rather than full realities. With Ghana's independence a great stirring began among the French Africans.

General de Gaulle, returning to power in 1958, quickly understood the situation and met it head-on with a dramatic offer. In a referendum that year he gave the territories a full range of choices. They could have complete independence, in which case France would withdraw completely and immediately. If they preferred to retain their association with France, they could unite with the mother country as overseas "departments," or they could keep their status as overseas territories, or become autonomous republics joined with France in a new, supranational grouping to be known as the French Community.

As members of this new Community they would be self-governing, but all matters of common concern—foreign policy, defense, currency, economic and financial planning, as well as strategic raw materials policy—would be handled by an executive council composed of the premiers of all the member states, presided over by the French president. If a member decided to withdraw and become fully sovereign and independent, it would be free to do so.

Accompanied by the prestigious and pro-Community Houphouët-Boigny, De Gaulle toured the African territories explaining the offer and building good will. The result was almost unanimous in favor of republican autonomy within the Community. The lone rebuff was from Guinea, led by Sékou Touré.

Touré was a militant young leftist and Pan-Africanist, the founder and leader of the powerful Union Générale des Travailleurs de l'Afrique Noire (its goal: "To unite and organize the workers of black Africa, to coordinate their trade union activities in the struggle against the colonial regime and all other forms of exploitation"). Touré had wanted the French territories to federate, declare independence and then—with the strength of their unity and liberty—drive a bargain with France. He had fought for these ideas within the R.D.A. party, of which he was a vice president, but had been defeated there by the older, more conservative Houphouët-Boigny. The latter was a pragmatist who was convinced that French cultural, technical and financial support would be needed for a long time to come, and hence that the best interests of the African territories lay in a close, voluntary association with France that would secure these benefits but allow each territory to decide for itself, as time went by, the political relationship it wanted with France and the others. Resentful of Houphouët-Boigny and suspicious of France and of De Gaulle, Touré announced, "We prefer poverty in liberty to riches in slavery," and led Guinea (by 97 per cent of its votes) into independence.

Guinea soon acquired the "poverty" of the slogan, for France's abrupt withdrawal brought economic chaos. But Guinea's "liberty" was equally conspicuous. Other French Africans watched, fascinated, as Touré visited Nkrumah and arranged a "union" of Guinea with Ghana (and a $28 million loan), secured financial and technical aid from the Communist countries, visited Washington and spoke in the U.N. General Assembly as the head of an independent state.

Partly from this influence, partly from the impatience that many other, younger men had

GHANA'S NATIONAL ANTHEM

Represented here are two stanzas of Ghana's national hymn, which evoke the new Africa's spirit of exhilaration.

Lift high the flag of Ghana,
The gay star shining in the sky,
Bright with the souls of our fathers,
Beneath whose shade we live and die!
Red for the blood of the heroes in the fight,
Green for the precious farms of our birthright,
And linked with these the shining golden band
That marks the richness of our Fatherland.

We'll live and die for Ghana,
Our land of hope for ages to come!
Shout it aloud, O Ghana,
   and beat it out upon the drum!
Come from the palm-lined shore, from the broad northern plain,
From the farm and the forest, the mountain and mine,
Your children sing with ancient minstrel lore:
Freedom for ever, for evermore!

felt even at the time the Community was formed —for many intermeshed reasons, but most of all because "independence" had become the emotionally charged symbol of the times—the autonomous republics began to exercise their option for independence. By the end of 1961 all of them had taken their places in the U.N. as sovereign nations. Today the Community still exists, but the relationships that the original members have with it now are various and subject to momentary change. French influence is still strong almost everywhere except in Guinea; but what began as a political community has become mainly, in Houphouët-Boigny's term, a "fraternal" one loosely bonded by common sentiment and self-interest.

THE chain reaction was bound to hit the Congo, blowing to smithereens the Belgian dream of gradualism. Belgian policy might have worked—but only if the Congo had been walled off from the rest of the world, existing in a political vacuum. And for some while, in fact, the officials in charge of Belgian colonial policy seemed to assume that there was such a vacuum. In 1955 Joseph Van Bilsen, a young professor of political science who had spent time in the Congo, published a report entitled "A Thirty-Year Plan for the Emancipation of Belgian Africa." It was the first serious proposal from a respected source that a timetable should be set for autonomy. The "Van Bilsen Plan" found backing among many Belgian liberals, and among literate, politically-minded Congolese it was received with enthusiasm. But to the Belgian business interests who had over two billion dollars invested in the Congo, and to colonial administrators, it seemed visionary and radical. Some day there would be autonomy, perhaps even independence; but the child must crawl before it walked, and walk before it ran—and 30 years was a short time.

The first tentative experiment, a closely supervised adventure in crawling, was tried in 1957. In three cities—Leopoldville, Jadotville and Elisabethville—the people of each commune or district were allowed indirectly to elect communal burgomasters, who were allowed to handle routine administrative duties in the commune. But the central administration of the city remained in the hands of the chief burgomaster, who was appointed by the governor general. The elections, the first in the Belgian Congo's history, went off on the whole very nicely. Only one of the popular choices was rejected by the government as unsuitable. There was a disturbing note when Joseph Kasavubu, on his inauguration as one of the Leopoldville burgomasters, made a speech urging that political rights be expanded rapidly; however, after reprimanding him the government allowed him to continue in office.

This was the meager beginning. Not of political discontent, for there had been plenty of that, but previously it had had only indirect outlets through tribal associations and other semisocial, cultural, religious or welfare groups. With elections, however, the Belgians had to allow political parties to come into existence. Consequently the groups could now become overtly political, and their leaders could become rallying symbols for the masses.

THE Congo elections occurred in the year of Ghana's independence, the year also when the *loi-cadre* took effect in the French territories. By the summer of 1958, De Gaulle was touring these same territories offering the wide choices already mentioned. His appearance in Brazzaville, a 20-minute ferry ride from Leopoldville, inspired a Leopoldville group to petition the government for a speed-up of political rights and, shortly afterward, to form the first national political party, the *Mouvement National Congolais*. The leader of its radical wing, which dominated the movement, was an eloquent and energetic young émigré from Stanleyville—a postal employee there until he was jailed for embezzlement, and subsequently the manager of a Leopoldville brewery —named Patrice Lumumba.

In December of that year an "All African Peoples' Conference" was held in Ghana, with Nkrumah's Convention People's Party as host.

Invitations had gone to political groups all over the continent, and the Belgians, conscious of the bad impression that would be created if they refused to allow any Congolese to attend, decided to let Congo politics be represented by the *Mouvement*, which at least had the virtue of a national, rather than tribal, outlook. Lumumba headed the small delegation.

ON his return from the Accra conference Lumumba, fired with Nkrumahian doctrines, spoke at an enthusiastic mass rally and raised the call for immediate independence. Seven days later, on January 4, 1959, rioting broke out in Leopoldville—and this was the beginning of the end. The Belgians tried repression. They promised rapid reforms. But nothing could stem the wild surge of revolt that swept the Congo. By January of 1960, Belgian and Congolese leaders were meeting in Brussels to work out independence terms, and the day was set: June 30. Instead of Van Bilsen's 30 years, the whole affair took three.

From complacency the Belgian attitude had progressed to misgiving to comprehension to alarm to panic; and the policy that had granted too little too late now gave too much too soon. The Republic of the Congo, unprepared for responsibility, lasted exactly five days before a mutiny of the Congolese army, or Force Publique, blew it up—with all the gruesome and fantastic consequences that a dismayed world has watched.

The uprising in Portuguese Angola, which followed less than nine months later, was nourished by many of the same sources. Its best-known leader, Holden Roberto, came from the part of the old Kingdom of Kongo that Portugal acquired during the colonial scramble—in fact his birthplace and boyhood home, the town of São Salvador, stands on the site of the old kingdom's capital and royal court. Mission-educated, Roberto went on to secondary school in the Belgian Congo, stayed to work in the government's financial division, and while stationed in Leopoldville became involved in the ABAKO movement for Kongo's rebirth.

There were many other Angolans in the Belgian part of the lower Congo, especially in Leopoldville, to which they had been attracted by the greater economic opportunities. In 1954, with some fellow émigrés, Roberto formed a clandestine independence group called Union of the Peoples of Angola. He was on hand in Leopoldville for the events of 1957 and 1958, and somehow he even managed to get to the All African Peoples' Conference in Ghana, returning, like Lumumba, full of fire and new plans. In March 1961, with supplies that presumably had been obtained from or by way of the newly independent Congo where his ABAKO colleague Kasavubu was president, and with a guerrilla force that included Angolans living and trained in the Congo, his group began a terroristic revolt in the northern part of the Portuguese colony.

AFTER six months of bloody fighting, in which some 1,000 Portuguese and 25,000 Africans were killed, Portuguese troops managed to contain the revolt and drive the remnants into hiding. As a consequence, however, Portugal was forced to re-examine its record in Africa, and late in 1961 it announced a long-range plan of education, enfranchisement and economic betterment for Angola and its other African "provinces." The basic policy of Assimilation remains, but now Portugal hopes to implement it at a pace that will make it mean something to the African masses. How successful this will be is anybody's guess. Looked at objectively, however, considering the spirit of the times and the lateness of the hour the chances for success would seem to be exceedingly poor.

From the foregoing, it should be clear that the dynamic forces of the African Revolution have formed patterns. But there have been static elements, too—elements of resistance and inertia—and these have also formed recognizable patterns. Tribal rulers and regional potentates have resisted—widely and sometimes violently, the extreme case being Moise Tshombe in the Congo's Katanga Province—the efforts of "nationalists" to subordinate their power and blend them into the newly-formed "nations." Ethnic, cultural and religious rivalries have also slowed the pace.

There are two other important elements—so important that, if they were plotted on a piece of graph paper, the correlations between the two curves might almost define the chances of success for nationalism in the various territories —"success" meaning the attainment of independence *and* internal stability. One of these elements is education: not just the amount of simple literacy, but—critically—the existence of a highly educated elite that has had training in the processes of orderly government and is prepared to assume political responsibility when independence arrives. The Gold Coast, which led the parade in British Africa, had the largest elite with the most experience. Similarly, it was Senegal and the Ivory Coast which furnished the early impetus and which also provided the most sophisticated leadership in the French territories.

THE other element is the "settler": especially the European, but also—in some instances even more important—the Asian. In west Africa there were few of either category who regarded themselves as permanent residents. There were comparatively few in the Belgian Congo or in the French areas to the north. But in Portuguese areas, and in British Central and East Africa, there are a great many people who, although regarded by the Africans as foreigners, consider Africa their permanent and rightful home. Numbers of them were born there, others have spent most of their lives there—and in the farms and ranches, the shops and businesses, the houses and cities that they have created, the whole pattern of their lives exists. And regardless of moral and legal issues past or present, emotionally they have been no more prepared to trust their destinies to African rule (particularly after the Congo debacle) than the early residents of Sioux City, Iowa, for instance, would have accepted equably the prospect of being ruled by the Sioux Indians.

They have resisted in proportion to their numbers, to their economic and political power, and to the degrees of their understanding, tolerance and optimism. In the U.N. Trusteeship Territories they could hope to achieve only a certain delay and some constitutional safeguards. In Tanganyika, where the government has been under the control of the extraordinarily able and far-sighted Julius Nyerere, the safeguards were given freely and still seem reasonably secure. In the non-U.N. territories, present attitudes among the settlers range from resignation and nervous acceptance of the inevitable to bristling defiance.

NYASALAND, with few settlers, already has internal autonomy under an African chief minister, Dr. Hastings Banda, and an African-controlled legislature. Northern Rhodesia has a new constitution which may yield a similar result within a few years. Uganda has constitutional guarantees for its sizable Asian populace, but a record of anti-Asian feeling that could make these guarantees a flabby shield indeed. Kenya, where the presence of the "white settlers" on much of the best land was a factor leading to the Mau Mau terror, moved toward independence beset with a host of problems stemming from bitter tribal rivalries.

In Angola and Mozambique, Assimilation on a new schedule is the "answer"—backed by Portuguese guns. In Southern Rhodesia, with a European population of 200,000 (vs. 2,900,000 Africans), "racial partnership" has been the white man's answer for years—and for years has been little more than a slogan. But recently there was a new "liberalized" version of it, too, which was immediately denounced by local African leaders. There had already been violence in Southern Rhodesia—and doubtless there would be more.

Uhuru! Freedom! Independence! From 1957 on, this was the shining, irresistible, all-consuming goal. In a flash of history, it had been largely attained. Only one question remained for those who had it.

The question was and is: "And *then* what?"

In semi-autonomous Nyasaland, fiery nationalist leader Hastings Banda sits at home receiving the worshipful stares of his followers.

Wayward Juggernaut of Nationalism

A single-minded drive, African nationalism has nevertheless produced a multitude of effects. It has created sturdy nations and spindly, moribund ones. It has imposed order on tribal anarchy and created chaos out of colonial order. It has embittered race relations and it has also helped improve them. But nationalism is less prominent as a creator than as a destroyer—one that is wiping out a tangle of institutions and powers that were expected to last forever.

*GHANA, first of the colonies
to become free,
has been a bellwether
of the independence movement*

EXULTANT TEARS are wiped (*opposite*) by Prime Minister (now President) Kwame Nkrumah as he hears Ghana proclaimed a sovereign nation.

TRIUMPHANT DANCE performed by Britain's Duchess of Kent and Nkrumah (*left*) was part of the cordial ceremony attending Ghana's placid birth.

YOUTH PARADE streams through Accra to welcome the Duchess of Kent, who represented the British crown as it surrendered control over its colony.

STURDY SQUIRE, a white farmer sits stolidly with his wife in their austerely baronial farmhouse in Kenya's "white highlands." A ruling minority who have been deeply entrenched for decades, Kenya's settlers are now returning to England by the thousands, driven by fear of a future in which Kenya's African majority will rule.

AGED MESSIAH, Jomo Kenyatta, once imprisoned for his part in the Mau Mau revolt, has an almost mystical hold on the loyalty of the Kikuyu, Kenya's largest tribe.

POLITICAL SOPHISTICATE, youthful Tom Mboya, a trade union leader whose support cuts across tribal divisions, has risen rapidly to political eminence in Kenya.

OMINOUS EXUBERANCE prompts a Congolese to snatch Belgian King Baudouin's sword on the day in 1960 when he came in "accord and friendship" to free the Congo. Within a week the riotous levity turned into bloody riots as the army turned on its white officers and old tribal feuds burst out to create chaos for 18 months.

THE CONGO has become a lurid kaleidoscope of bloodshed and anarchy since its abrupt rise to freedom

TRIBAL TROUBLEMAKERS are rounded up by Congolese security troops (*above*) after a post-independence flare-up of feuding. A few days later the troops themselves erupted in revolt against all authority—civil and military. They became a runaway force that split into disorderly bands and smashed the Congo's frail unity.

WILY SECESSIONIST Moise Tshombe is greeted by Belgians (*right*) who back his militant drive to keep copper-rich Katanga Province out of the Congo's control.

TATTERED REBELS drill in a village in northern Angola (*above*), home base of an insurrection which broke out early in 1961. Stirred by the turbulence in the neighboring Congo, terrorists murdered scores of Portuguese settlers.

GRIM OFFICIALS attend an ill-fated funeral (*opposite*) in Luanda for men of both races killed by rebels. When some Africans made a disturbance nearby, Portuguese went wild, beating and killing every African they could find.

FRENZIED POLICE, swept up by the furor at the funeral, join the hunt for Africans (*below*). During the first six months of insurrection, rebels killed some 1,000 whites, and the Portuguese in retaliation killed 25,000 Africans.

10

Problems and Obstacles Ahead

THE new Africa—paraphrasing a geological description used in the beginning of this book—consists largely of a solid mass of problems laid down in the course of thousands of years and suddenly uplifted. It is surrounded by seas of doubt and filled with extraordinary contrasts: peaks of integrity and oozy swamps of expediency, jungles of ignorance, fear and suspicion and splendid vistas of knowledge, hope and brotherhood. Out of this disordered scene will come—nobody can say what. But, as surely as modern Africa reflects the past, the Africa yet-to-be is already contained in the present. And, while eschewing discoveries and

prophecies, we can profit by reconnoitering this landscape and spotting what seem to be its major features, the main questions whose answers will shape the future.

Perhaps the most important question of all is Pan-Africanism. A United States of Africa would not in itself dispose of Africa's difficulties, any more than federal unity disposed of all the problems of the original 13 American states. But it would help immensely. In a proportionately lesser degree, Africa would be better off if it had closely allied or cooperating groups of countries. Most African leaders accept this principle, and numerous efforts have been and are continuing to be made to give it substance.

In 1961, twelve of the former French territories, after arranging themselves in a variety of combinations (including a full-fledged union between Senegal and Mali, which fissioned after only three months), formed the African-Malagasy Union, which links them in a loose political and economic alliance. Guinea and Mali, which did not participate, meanwhile had allied themselves with Ghana, Morocco, the United Arab Republic and the provisional government of Algeria. This alliance grew out of a conference held earlier at Casablanca, and the members are known as the "Casablanca group." Later that same year, there was a conference at Monrovia, Liberia, to try to establish a closer relationship among the former French, Belgian and British territories. The "Casablanca group" declined to send any representatives but most of the other new nations did, and these became known as the "Monrovia group."

BOTH groups believe in African unity, but differ sharply about the means to achieve it. The "Casablanca" approach is political: federate all the governments immediately, then work out the practical problems of integrating the countries. The "Monrovia" idea is to begin from the bottom, with economic and social cooperation, and build toward political merger. In January 1962 at Lagos, Nigeria, 20 countries met to organize this cooperative effort.

Either way, however, there are great obstacles to African unity. Some derive from the colonial heritage: differences in legal systems, currencies, communications and all the rest of the apparatus of government and economy; differences in perspective among the educated elite who retain not only the language but much of the cultural outlook of those who educated them.

Other obstacles derive from the new independence. Self-government was the great target in the old days, "Freedom!" the great slogan, and it is not easy to shift gears suddenly to the much more abstract idea of unity.

For the governing elite, moreover, the sovereignty of the nation has in many cases brought highly satisfying individual benefits: good salaries, perquisites such as houses and cars and servants; the pleasures of travel, and the prestige of titles, of diplomatic posts and of voting and speaking at the United Nations. To pool sovereignty would, in many cases, mean to lose status—and perhaps much else, a prospect that appeals to the officials of Africa no more than to those in other parts of the world.

ACCORDINGLY, in the absence of a miracle, the new states of Africa are likely to hold fast to a large measure of individual sovereignty for some time to come. This does not preclude the possibility of individual unions or of more or less effective cooperation—customs unions, cultural exchanges, political alliances, and so forth—among neighbors or even large groupings of countries. But most of the nations evidently intend to stand—divided. And this invites weaknesses and troubles.

In particular, trouble may arise over the question of borders. The colonial scramble separated numerous tribes and ethnically or culturally homogeneous groups by borders that are now the borders of new states. In most parts of Tropical Africa, tribal loyalties are still very strong—often far stronger than loyalties to the new nations. These peoples want to be reunited, and the borders still stand in their way.

The problem exists widely and in varying degrees of seriousness, perhaps most acutely among the Ewe, divided between Ghana and Togo; the Bakongo of the lower Congo River, split three ways; the Masai of Kenya and Tanganyika (under British rule they roamed freely back and forth and will insist on continuing to do so); and the Somali.

Another important factor is that many peoples who were grouped together under colonial rule would now like to be responsible again for their own affairs. Some, like those of Buganda, have felt this way because they have strong "national" traditions of their own; others because, in varying degrees, they dislike and mistrust their neighbors. For instance, there is a strong movement among the Nilotic tribes of the southern part of the Republic of the Sudan to detach themselves from the Arabized north. An even more acute example presents itself in Kenya, where a number of smaller tribes have pressed for local autonomy, fearing that the two very large and politically allied tribes, the Luo and the Kikuyu, would control the government of an independent Kenya and run it in ways inimical to their interests. In scores if not hundreds of other instances, tribal groups would fracture the new and emerging nations if they could.

This has considerable bearing on the question of democracy. The term "democratic government" means different things to different people. But as it is used in the United States and most western nations, it requires at least one precondition for successful functioning: those who are being governed, even though they may argue about methods, pace and many other things, must have at least a general, tacit understanding of what the main goals are and a similar tacit agreement to seek these goals by orderly processes. Where tribal loyalties and ambitions are strong this elementary condition does not exist, for one cannot rationally try to put a nation together and at the same time try to pull it apart into autonomous units.

WHEN to tribalism are added religious rivalries (as among Moslems, Christians and pagans), cultural antagonisms (as between pastoralists and cultivators), a vast illiteracy, a wide belief that worldly events are controlled by occult forces, social concepts as diverse as Marxism, feudalism and village communalism, social groups as various as the university-educated elite, rootless urban proletarians and tradition-bound rural masses, a communication problem based on so fundamental a matter as lack of a common language; and then in addition to all this there is added a strong tradition of personal leadership, the idea that the chief—emir, king, whatever his titles and duties might be—personifies the tribe or state, and hence that open opposition to him is in a sense both irreligious and treasonable—in such conditions

the chances, to say the least, do not favor parliamentary democracy.

As Kwame Nkrumah noted in 1956, before Ghana's independence, "Even a system based on social justice and a democratic constitution may need backing up, during the period following independence, by emergency measures of a totalitarian kind." The remark seems especially prescient: the measures he has used have caused many people to fear that Ghana is becoming a totalitarian state.

WHAT has so far proved to be possible in a fair number of the new countries is what some of the Africans call "one-party democracy": a degree of discussion and joint decision-making by the upper leadership of whatever nationalist organization did the most to bring about independence and thereby emerged in control of the new government. In this special and limited sense, democracy may well survive and perhaps evolve into something closer to the western idea. But for the present and near future, while Africans are coping with the difficulties of building nations from dissident and ambitious small-scale societies, firm central control—whether under single party rule or the rule of a Leader—is likely to prevail.

This, in turn, relates closely to the question of what kind of economic and social systems the new countries will have. All of them are "underdeveloped nations," some of them merely less so than others. Living standards are low; and, with the attainment of independence, expectations for betterment are high. It is difficult to make dramatic economic progress under the private-capital system—especially when, as is true in most of the new countries, there is a meager amount of capital in private hands and only the government, using its taxing powers, can possibly accumulate enough to finance large projects. To this, one can add that traditional African ways of life have been largely "social" or "communal," and that among the African educated elite a great number (probably a large majority) subscribe to socialism in one form or another as a political doctrine.

163

Problems and Obstacles Ahead

On the surface, at least, this is a situation that would seem to present rich opportunities for the U.S.S.R. and China and other Communist nations. And indeed they have been busy in Africa, opening embassies, offering economic and technical aid, inviting political leaders to their capitals, granting scholarships to entice African students to their universities, and funneling money into propaganda agencies and into the hands of politicians and factions whom they hope to use as instruments of conquest.

THE Communists have an extremely useful psychological weapon, too—and they use it in Africa and at the United Nations—in their pious "anti-colonialism." They demand that all "colonialism," "imperialism," "capitalistic exploitation" be abolished forthwith, and they warn that economic aid from the former colonial powers (or from the U.S., with whom those powers are allied in the North Atlantic Treaty Organization) will bring about an indirect but still effective domination, a "neo-colonialism." Also—although local parties have been weak or non-existent—Communism's assets include a sizable sprinkling (especially in the former French territories) of African leaders who were trained in Marxism-Leninism in their university days in Europe, and others who at one time became Communist allies or close sympathizers during the struggles of the independence movement.

With such factors at work, and with Africa now fully exposed to all the ideas, economic forces and political crosscurrents swirling in the world at large, it would be foolish to expect that the new nations can be isolated from the Cold War as some wishful thinkers both in Africa and in the West have hoped. But it would be equally unrealistic to conclude, in the words of Sir Roy Welensky, Prime Minister of the Federation of Rhodesia and Nyasaland, that "the unbridled African nationalism of today . . . suits the Communist book to the last letter." Both the political orientation of the African nations in world affairs and the direction taken by their internal social-economic systems can be influenced very powerfully—perhaps decisively—by the actions and attitudes of the West.

The actions that are called for are primarily economic. To diversify their trade, which now in most cases is dependent on one or two basic commodities (Ghana's cocoa, Ethiopia's coffee, etc.), and to build the roads, power stations, airports, medical services and, above all, the schools upon which their future development depends, they need capital and technical assistance.

The Africans are not inclined to be too choosy about the sources: as Kwame Nkrumah has said, "It doesn't matter where you go for your aid. If you can get it, *get* it." But for many reasons of convenience—their use of western languages and currencies, for instance, and the relative inexperience of China and the Soviet Union in African affairs—most of them would prefer that it came from the West. Most are well aware, however, that aid from western governments, essential though that is, cannot do the whole job. Private capital will also be needed. And they know they can attract it only by supplying the conditions that will make profit possible, as well as by meaningful legal guarantees against expropriation.

THEIR eagerness for western development aid is qualified by two provisos. Aid should carry no political strings. And private investors must operate with a sense of public responsibility—with a concern not just for making money, but also for the welfare of their African employees and of the country; further, in some cases the investors must agree to African participation in management, stockholdings and profits. In short, the white man, with his money and skills, will be welcome as a collaborator and as an equal, but never again as a superior.

The responsible leaders in Africa know the difficulties ahead. They are determined to find a solution. They are equally determined that this solution will not be imposed on them by outsiders. Whatever it turns out to be, it will be something new, different and African.

Youngsters in Ghana cluster around a village political debater. Next page: Kenyans rally to support their leader Jomo Kenyatta.

DETERMINED to prove themselves fully independent and beholden to no one . . .

. . . Africans passionately insist that their days of passivity and subjection are

over and that they intend to construct their bold new world in their own manner

Appendix

HISTORICAL DATES

500 B.C.-A.D. 1415: PERIOD BEFORE EUROPEAN CONTACT

c.500 B.C. Hanno, a Carthaginian, makes first voyage to west Africa and explores the Sierra Leone area

c.A.D. 300 First African kingdom, Ghana, arises in the Sudan; lasts until about 1200

c.700 Arabs begin colonization of east African coast and organization of slave trade on a large scale

1009 Songhai tribe in the Sudan converted to Islam; Moslems begin to ship Negro slaves to Europe

1100 City of Timbuktu founded by Songhai merchants. By the 14th Century it is a flourishing trade center of the western Sudan

1307-1332 Islamic Mali Empire at height of power under its ruler Kankan Musa. It controls the entire western Sudan

1415-1769: PERIOD OF UNRESTRICTED SLAVE TRADE

1441 Portuguese mariners Tristão and Gonçalves reach Cape Blanc, take back a dozen slaves to Portugal

1448 First European trading post in west Africa is established at Arguin island off Cape Blanc by Portuguese

1482-1484 Diogo Cão, Portuguese explorer, reaches mouth of the Congo

1493 Songhai Empire, successor to Mali as leading power of the Sudan, achieves apex as Mohammed Askia mounts throne

1493-1528 First African universities are established under Mohammed Askia

1497-1499 Vasco da Gama sails around the southern tip of Africa to India

1502-1510 Portuguese gain control of east African coast from Arabs

1562 First British venture in slave trade

1598 First Dutch trading post on Gold Coast. Dutch gain commercial supremacy on west coast in next 40 years

1618 First British fort in west Africa constructed on St. James Island

1642 French begin the colonization of Madagascar

1652 First Dutch settlement established on Cape of Good Hope

1665 British capture Dutch forts on Gold Coast

1677-1678 French capture the Dutch stations in Senegal

1698-1699 Imam of Oman captures Mombasa, Zanzibar, Pemba and Kilwa from Portuguese

1737 First translation of the Bible into an African language (Fanti)

1769-1919: PERIOD OF EXPLORATION, PARTITION, CESSATION OF SLAVE TRADE

1769-1772 James Bruce initiates modern exploration of Africa with travels in Ethiopia and eastern Sudan, discovering source of Blue Nile

1772 Slavery declared illegal in Britain

1787 400 freed Negroes settled under British auspices in Sierra Leone

1794 First national act of the United States against the slave trade. French Revolutionary Convention declares against slavery

1795-1805 Mungo Park, Scottish explorer, leads two expeditions to trace the Niger River, dies during second expedition

1804-1810 Fulani leader Othman dan Fodio rallies faithful, launches holy war and conquers Hausa states of Northern Nigeria

1815 European powers confer on African colonies at the Congress of Vienna and decry slave trade

1817 France prohibits slave trade

1821 First American Negro colonists land in Liberia under auspices of the American Colonization Society

1822 British expedition under Hugh Clapperton crosses the Sahara, explores the Lake Chad region

1833 Britain forbids slavery in colonies

1847 Liberia becomes an independent nation

1852-1856 Dr. David Livingstone of Britain journeys across southern Africa

1856-1859 Richard Burton and John Speke explore Lake Tanganyika

1874-1877 Henry M. Stanley, an American journalist, travels to Lakes Victoria and Tanganyika, explores the Congo River

1875-1880 Count Savorgnan de Brazza explores the area north of the Congo River for France

1883 First German colony in Africa is established at Angra Pequena (present-day South-West Africa)

1884-1885 The Berlin Conference of European powers recognizes Congo Free State, pledges improvements in colonies and declares that annexation must be accompanied by effective occupation

1889-1892 War between French and Dahomey won by the French

1893-1898 French occupy Djenné and Timbuktu, gain control over Songhai

1895 French establish a protectorate in Madagascar

1896-1900 Last of seven British-Ashanti wars establishes British rule in Gold Coast

1897 British conquer Benin

1899 Joint rule established over the Sudan by Britain and Egypt

1908 Congo Free State becomes a Belgian colony under rule of Belgian parliament after 24 years of personal rule by King Leopold II

1914 British amalgamate colony of Lagos and protectorates of Northern and Southern Nigeria

1919-1945: PERIOD OF TRUSTEESHIP

1919 Trusteeships set up under League of Nations: German East Africa mandated to Britain, Ruanda-Urundi to Belgium, South-West Africa to South Africa; Cameroons and Togo divided between Britain and France

1923-1924 Southern Rhodesia chooses self-government under the British Crown; Northern Rhodesia becomes British protectorate

1935-1936 Italy conquers Ethiopia

1941 Italians driven from Ethiopia

1945-PRESENT: PERIOD OF NATIONALISM AND INDEPENDENCE

1945 League of Nations mandates become trust territories under the United Nations

1951 First general elections in Gold Coast; Kwame Nkrumah becomes first native African head of government under colonial rule

1952 Federation is established among Northern Rhodesia, Southern Rhodesia and Nyasaland. Mau Mau rebellion in Kenya begins

1953 Self-government granted the Sudan by Britain and Egypt; first general elections held

1957 Ghana becomes the first African nation to gain its independence from a modern colonial power and the first Negro-ruled member of the British Commonwealth

1958 Coup d'état in the Sudan, military government formed. Conference of independent African states meets in Accra, Ghana. France holds referendum for African colonies in which Guinea is the only one to vote for immediate independence

1960 Cameroon, Togo, Malagasy, Republic of the Congo, Somalia, Dahomey, Niger, Upper Volta, Ivory Coast, Chad, Central African Republic, Congo Republic, Gabon, Mali, Senegal, Nigeria, Mauritania attain independence

1961 Tanganyika and Sierra Leone become independent

FOR FURTHER READING

CHAPTER ONE: THE LAND

Beaver, Stanley H., and L. Dudley Stamp, *A Regional Geography*. Longmans, Green, 1952.

Burton, Richard F., *The Lake Regions of Central Africa*. Horizon Press, 1961.

Dinesen, Isak, *Out of Africa*. Modern Library, 1937.

Gide, André, *Travels in the Congo*. Alfred A. Knopf, 1929.

Gourau, Pierre, *The Tropical World*. Longmans, Green, 1961.

Hickman, G. M., and W. H. G. Dickins, *The Lands and Peoples of East Africa*. Longmans, Green, 1960.

Kimble, George H. T., *Tropical Africa*. Twentieth Century Fund, 1960.

Light, Richard U., *Focus on Africa*. American Geographical Society, 1941.

Post, van der, Laurens, *The Lost World of the Kalahari*. William Morrow, 1958.

Richards, P. W., *The Tropical Rain Forest*. Cambridge University Press, 1957.

Stamp, L. Dudley, *Africa, A Study in Tropical Development*. John Wiley and Sons, 1953.

Tilman, Harold W., *Snow on the Equator*. Macmillan, 1938.

Worthington, S., and B. E., *Inland Waters of Africa*. Macmillan, 1933.

CHAPTER TWO: TRIBES AND PEOPLES

Greenberg, Joseph H., *Studies in African Linguistic Classification*. Compass, 1955.

Hailey, Lord W. M., *An African Survey*. Oxford University Press, 1957.

Kenyatta, Jomo, *Facing Mount Kenya; The Tribal Life of the Gikuyu*. British Book Centre, Inc., 1956.

Seligman, C. G., *Races of Africa*. Oxford University Press, 1957.

South African Institute of International Affairs, *Africa South of the Sahara*. Oxford University Press, 1951.

Turnbull, Colin, *Forest People*. Simon & Schuster, 1961.

Westermann, Diedrich, *The African Today and Tomorrow*. Oxford University Press, 1949.

CHAPTER THREE: MIGRATIONS AND SETTLEMENT

Churchill, Winston, *My African Journey*. George H. Doran, 1908.

Leakey, L. S. B., *Stone Age Africa*. Oxford University Press, 1936.

Murdock, George P., *Africa; Its Peoples and Their Culture History*. McGraw-Hill, 1959.

Ottenberg, Simon and Phoebe, *Cultures and Societies of Africa*. Random House, 1960.

Wieschhoff, H. A., *Africa*. University Museum Bulletin, University of Pennsylvania Press, 1945.

CHAPTER FOUR: ANCIENT KINGDOMS

Arkell, A. J., *A History of the Sudan*. University of London, The Athlone Press, 1955.

Bovill, E. W., *Caravans of the Old Sahara*. Oxford University Press, 1933.

Davidson, Basil, *The Lost Cities of Africa*. Little, Brown, 1959.

Fage, J. D., *An Introduction to the History of West Africa*. Cambridge University Press, 1955.

Graft-Johnson, J. C. de, *African Glory*. Frederick A. Praeger, 1955.

Middleton, John, and David Tait, ed., *Tribes without Rulers*. Routledge and Kegan Paul, London, 1958.

Perham, Margery, *The Government of Ethiopia*. Faber and Faber, London, 1958.

Reusch, Richard, *History of East Africa*. Frederick Ungar, 1961.

Steindorff, George, and Keith C. Steele, *When Egypt Ruled the East*. University of Chicago Press, 1957.

CHAPTER FIVE: THE SLAVE TRADE

Coupland, R., *The Exploitation of East Africa, 1856-1890*. Faber and Faber, London, 1939.

Davidson, Basil, *Black Mother*. Little, Brown, 1961.

Forde, Daryll, ed., *Efik Traders of Old Calabar*. Oxford University Press, 1954.

Herskovits, Melville J., *The Myth of the Negro Past*. Beacon Press, 1958.

Moorehead, Alan, *The White Nile*. Harper & Bros., 1960.

Morel, E. D., *The Black Man's Burden*. B. W. Huebsch, 1920.

Russell, H., *Human Cargoes*. Longmans, Green, 1948.

Stanley, Henry M., *Slavery and the Slave Trade in Africa*. Harper & Bros., 1893.

Wyndham, H. A., *The Atlantic and Slavery*. Oxford University Press, 1935.

CHAPTER SIX: AFRICA'S GODS

Evans-Pritchard, E. E., *Witchcraft, Oracles and Magic among the Azande*. Clarendon Press, 1937.

Frazer, James, *Golden Bough*. St. Martin's, 1955.

Freud, Sigmund, *Totem and Taboo*. W. W. Norton, 1952.

Malinowski, Bronislaw, *Magic, Science and Religion*. Doubleday, 1954.

Parrinder, Geoffrey, *African Traditional Religion*. Hutchinson's University Library, 1959.

Smith, Edwin W., ed., *African Ideas of God: A Symposium*. Edinburgh House Press, London, 1950.

Trimingham, John Spencer, *Islam in Ethiopia*. Oxford University Press, 1952.

——, *Islam in the Sudan*. Oxford University Press, 1949.

——, *Islam in West Africa*. Clarendon Press, 1959.

Webster, Hutton, *Magic*. Stanford University Press, 1948.

CHAPTER SEVEN: ART AND CULTURE

Bascom, W. R., and Paul Gebauer, *Handbook of West African Art*. Milwaukee Public Museum Popular Science Handbook Series 5, 1953.

Bleek, Dorothea F., *Cave Artists of South Africa*. Balkema, Capetown, 1953.

Caton-Thompson, G., *The Zimbabwe Culture: Ruins and Reactions*. Clarendon Press, 1931.

Elisofon, Eliot, and William Fagg, *The Sculpture of Africa*. Frederick A. Praeger, 1958.

Fortes, Meyer, *Oedipus and Job in West African Religion*. Cambridge University Press, 1959.

Paver, B., *Zimbabwe Cavalcade*. South Africa Central News Agency, Ltd., 1950.

Wieschhoff, H. A., *The Zimbabwe-Monomotapa Culture in South East Africa*. General Series in Anthropology, 8, 1941.

Wingert, Paul S., *The Sculpture of Negro Africa*. Columbia University Press, 1950.

CHAPTER EIGHT: COLONIALISM

Adam, Thomas R., *Government and Politics in Africa South of the Sahara*. Random House, 1959.

Buell, Raymond L., *The Native Problem in Africa*. Macmillan, 1928.

Duffy, James, *Portuguese Africa*. Harvard University Press, 1959.

Emerson, Rupert, *From Empire to Nation*. Harvard University Press, 1960.

Gunther, John, *Inside Africa*. Harper & Bros., 1955.

Hodgkin, Thomas, *Nationalism in Colonial Africa*. New York University Press, 1957.

International African Institute, *Social Implications of Industrialization and Urbanization in Africa South of the Sahara*. UNESCO, 1956.

Jahoda, Gustav, *White Man: A Study of the Attitudes of Africans to Europeans in Ghana before Independence*. Oxford University Press, 1961.

Joelson, F. S., ed., *Rhodesia and East Africa*. East Africa, Ltd., London, 1958.

Macmillan, W. M., *Africa Emergent*. Penguin Books, 1949.

Middleton, Lamar, *The Rape of Africa*. Harrison Smith and Robert Haas, 1936.

Oldham, J. H., *New Hope in Africa*. Longmans, Green, 1955.

Smith, Prudence, ed., *Africa in Transition*. Max Reinhardt, London, 1958.

Thompson, Virginia, and Richard Adloff, *French West Africa*. Stanford University Press, 1957.

Thurnwald, Richard C., *Black and White in East Africa*. G. Routledge & Sons, London, 1935.

Townsend, Mary E., *European Colonial Expansion since 1871*. J. B. Lippincott, 1941.

Wieschhoff, H. A., *Colonial Policies in Africa*. University of Pennsylvania Press, 1944.

CHAPTERS NINE AND TEN:
THE INDEPENDENCE MOVEMENT

Cameron, James, *The African Revolution*. Random House, 1961.

Coleman, James S., *Nigeria: Background to Nationalism*. University of California Press, 1958.

Cowan, L. Gray, *Local Government in West Africa*. Columbia University Press, 1958.

Delf, George, *Jomo Kenyatta*. Doubleday, 1961.

Duffy, James, and Robert A. Manners, *Africa Speaks*. D. Van Nostrand, 1961.

Haines, C. Grove, ed., *Africa Today*. Johns Hopkins Press, 1955.

Hatch, John, *Everyman's Africa*. Dennis Dobson, London, 1959.

Hempstone, Smith, *Africa—Angry Young Giant*. Frederick A. Praeger, 1961.

Horrabin, J. F., *An Atlas of Africa*. Frederick A. Praeger, 1960.

Hughes, John, *The New Face of Africa*. Longmans, Green, 1961.

Melady, Thomas Patrick, *Profiles of African Leaders*. Macmillan, 1961.

Segal, Ronald, *Political Africa; A Who's Who of Personalities and Parties*. Frederick A. Praeger, 1961.

Stillman, Calvin W., ed., *Africa in the Modern World*. University of Chicago Press, 1955.

POLITICAL UNITS IN TROPICAL AFRICA (as of December 31, 1961)

NAME	POP.	AREA (sq. mi.)	CAPITAL	GOVERNMENT
INDEPENDENT NATIONS				
Cameroon (includes former Southern Cameroons)	4,154,000	163,332	Yaoundé	French possession until 1960, now a republic
Central African Republic	1,224,000	227,118	Bangui	French possession until 1960, now a republic
Chad	2,541,000	446,640	Fort Lamy	French possession until 1960, now a republic
Congo Republic	816,000	125,890	Brazzaville	French possession until 1960, now a republic
Republic of the Congo	13,732,000	905,329	Leopoldville	Belgian colony until 1960, now a republic
Dahomey	1,750,000	44,713	Porto Novo	French possession until 1960, now a republic
Ethiopia (includes Eritrea)	21,351,000	457,147	Addis Ababa	Independent since 19th Century except for Italian rule 1885-1889 and 1935-1941; now a monarchy
Gabon	434,400	98,283	Libreville	French possession until 1960, now a republic
Ghana (includes former British Togo)	4,847,000	91,819	Accra	British possession until 1957, now a republic
Guinea	2,667,000	94,945	Conakry	French possession until 1958, now a republic
Ivory Coast	3,145,000	124,550	Abidjan	French possession until 1960, now a republic
Liberia	1,350,000	42,989	Monrovia	Republic
Malagasy Republic	5,225,000	228,510	Tananarive	French possession until 1960, now a republic
Mali (former Sudan)	3,748,000	465,050	Bamako	French possession until 1960, now a republic

NAME	POP.	AREA (sq. mi.)	CAPITAL	GOVERNMENT
INDEPENDENT NATIONS (cont.)				
Mauritania	685,000	419,390	Nouakchott	French possession until 1960, now a republic
Niger	2,515,000	459,180	Niamey	French possession until 1960, now a republic
Nigeria (includes northern Cameroons)	34,267,000	366,872	Lagos	British possession until 1960, now a republic
Senegal	2,337,000	76,153	Dakar	French possession until 1960, now a republic
Sierra Leone	2,185,000	27,925	Freetown	British colony until 1961, now a republic
Somalia (includes British Somaliland)	2,047,000	246,137	Mogadiscio	Italian and British possessions until 1960, now a single republic
Sudan	11,549,000	967,248	Khartoum	Under joint British-Egyptian rule until 1957, now a military dictatorship
Tanganyika	9,052,000	362,688	Dar es Salaam	British Trust Territory until 1961, now a republic
Togo	1,137,000	22,002	Lomé	French possession until 1960, now a republic
Upper Volta	3,516,000	105,879	Ougadougou	French possession until 1960, now a republic
BRITISH POSSESSIONS				
Bechuanaland	368,000	274,928	Lobatsi	Protectorate
Gambia	307,000	3,978	Bathurst	Colony and protectorate
Kenya	6,444,000	224,960	Nairobi	Colony and protectorate
Northern Rhodesia	2,430,000	288,130	Lusaka	Protectorate
Nyasaland	2,830,000	37,374	Zomba	Protectorate
Southern Rhodesia	3,070,000	150,333	Salisbury	Self-governing colony
Uganda	5,892,000	93,981	Entebbe	Protectorate
Zanzibar (includes Pemba)	304,000	1,020	Zanzibar	Protectorate ruled by Sultan
PORTUGUESE POSSESSIONS				
Angola	4,496,000	481,226	Luanda	Overseas province
Mozambique	6,253,000	297,654	Lourenço Marques	Overseas province
Portuguese Guinea	563,000	13,944	Bissau	Overseas province
FRENCH POSSESSION				
French Somaliland	69,000	8,494	Djibouti	Overseas territory
BELGIAN POSSESSION				
Ruanda-Urundi	4,901,000	20,916	Usumbura	Trust territory
SPANISH POSSESSION				
Spanish Guinea	216,000	10,828	Santa Isabel	Spanish province

Credits

The sources for the illustrations in this book are shown below. Credits for pictures from left to right are separated by commas, top to bottom by dashes.

Cover—Marilyn Silverstone from Nancy Palmer Agency
8, 9—Albert Fenn
10, 11—Maps by Bill Dove
17—Emil Schulthess from Black Star
18, 19—Alfred Eisenstaedt
20, 21—Eliot Elisofon, Emil Schulthess from Black Star
22, 23—Brian Brake from Magnum; except bottom left Marilyn Silverstone from Nancy Palmer Agency
24, 25—Eliot Elisofon
26, 27—Pete Turner from Free Lance Photographers Guild —Maitland Edey, James Whitmore for TIME
28—Eliot Elisofon
32, 33—Drawings by Burt Silverman
36—Larry Burrows, Terence Spencer
37, 38, 39—Eliot Elisofon
40—James Whitmore for TIME
41—Marc and Evelyne Bernheim from Rapho-Guillumette
42—Der Stern from Black Star; except top right Marc and Evelyne Bernheim from Rapho-Guillumette
43—Alfred Eisenstaedt
44, 45—N. R. Farbman
49—Map by Bill Dove
53—Ylla from Rapho-Guillumette
54, 55—James Burke
56 through 61—Eliot Elisofon
62—Alfred Eisenstaedt
67—Radio Times Hulton Picture Library
70—Myroslav Andrew Maksymiec
71, 72, 73—Alfred Eisenstaedt
74, 75—James Burke, Dominique Berretty from Europress, Larry Burrows
76, 77—Terence Spencer
78—*A Description of the Coasts of North and South Guinea and of Ethiopia Interior, vulgarly Angola, being a new and accurate account of the Western Maritime Countries of Africa* by John Barbot published 1732, courtesy Picton Library, Liverpool
82—Bibliothèque Nationale, Paris
85—Reproduced from the Collection of the Library of Congress

86—Basil Davidson
87—Painting by Stevan Dohanos
88—Painting by Robert Riggs
89—bottom courtesy the Marines Museum, Newport News, Va.
90, 91—Culver Pictures
92, 93—Ed Van Der Elsken from Black Star
100—Eliot Elisofon
101—W. Eugene Smith
102, 103—Harrison Forman, Courtesy Nigerian Information Service, New York—Paul Conklin from Pix
104—Ed Van Der Elsken from Black Star
105—Larry Burrows
106, 107—Eliot Elisofon
108—George Rodger from Magnum
116, 117—Larry Burrows
118, 119—Pierre Boulat courtesy Mission L'hote
120—Aldo Van Eyck
122, 123—Walker Evans © 1935, The Museum of Modern Art, New York
124—Carl Mydans
130—From *Flags of the World* courtesy Frederick Warne & Co. Ltd., London
133—Mark Kauffman
134—Homer Page from Magnum for FORTUNE—Erich Lessing from Magnum for FORTUNE
135—Kryn Taconis from Magnum
136, 137—Eliot Elisofon
138, 139—James Whitmore for TIME, Eliot Elisofon—Pete Turner from Free Lance Photographers Guild
140—Marilyn Silverstone from Nancy Palmer Agency
141—Dominique Berretty
142, 143—Larry Burrows
151—Terence Spencer
152, 153—Mark Kauffman
154, 155—Alfred Eisenstaedt, Terence Spencer—John Moss from Black Star
156, 157—Robert Lebeck, Larry Burrows—Terence Spencer
158, 159—James Burke; except top left Wide World Photos
160—Terence Spencer
165—Mark Kauffman
166, 167—Robert Coughlan

ACKNOWLEDGMENTS

The editors of this book are indebted to Professor William O. Brown, Professor Daniel F. McCall and Dr. Norman R. Bennett of the African Studies Program at Boston University, all of whom read and commented on portions of the text. Valuable assistance was also rendered by Colin M. Turnbull, Assistant Curator of African Ethnology of the American Museum of Natural History.

Mr. Coughlan is particularly grateful for the guidance given to him in his earlier writings on Africa by the late Dr. Heinrich A. Wieschhoff. As a pioneering scholar and teacher of African studies at the University of Pennsylvania, and later as a key adviser on African affairs to Secretary-General Dag Hammarskjöld of the United Nations, Dr. Wieschhoff had an important influence on contemporary African history. On September 17, 1961, he died in an air crash at Ndola, Northern Rhodesia, with the Secretary-General and 13 others while on a U.N. mission to bring peace to the Congo. Mr. Coughlan was then in Africa gathering materials for this text, which, of course, Dr. Wieschhoff did not live to see. The wisdom and friendship which he shared with Mr. Coughlan before his tragic death were, however, of inestimable value in the preparation of this book.

Index

This symbol in front of a page number indicates a photograph or painting of the subject mentioned.

Production staff for Time Incorporated

Arthur R. Murphy (Vice President and Director of Production)

Robert E. Foy, James P. Menton and Caroline Ferri

Text photocomposed on Photon equipment

under the direction of Albert J. Dunn and Arthur J. Dunn

x

Printed by R. R. Donnelley & Sons Company, Crawfordsville, Indiana,

and The Safran Printing Company, Detroit, Michigan

Bound by R. R. Donnelley & Sons Company, Crawfordsville, Indiana

Paper by The Mead Corporation, Dayton, Ohio

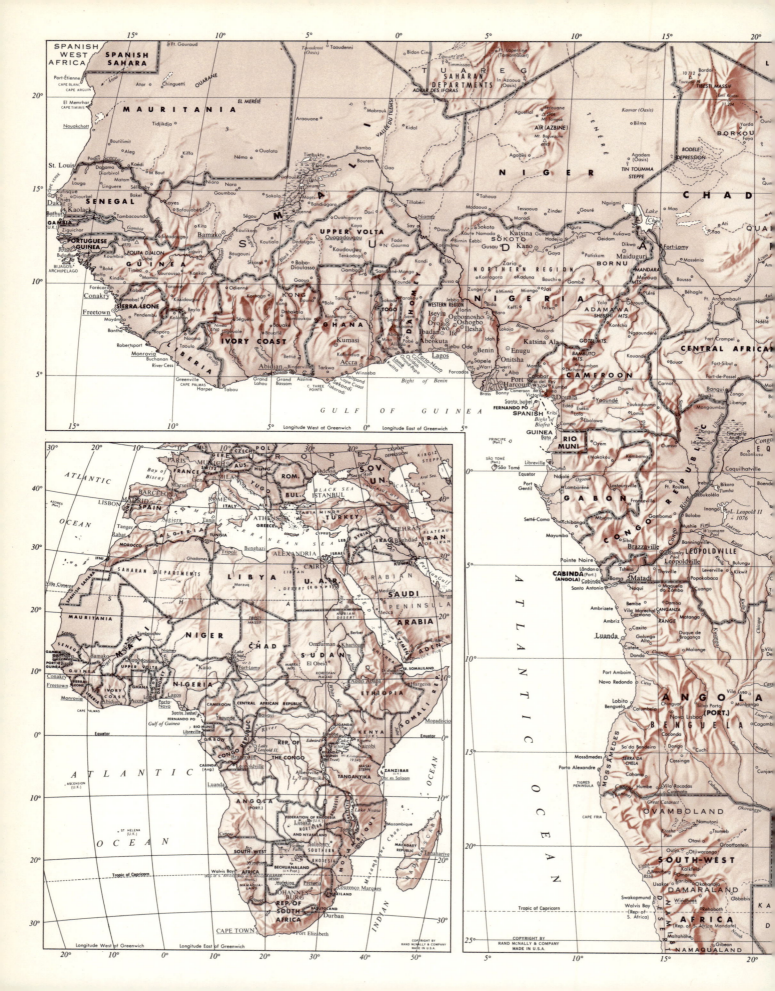